FREE DVD  **FREE DVD**

ASTB DVD from Trivium Test Prep!

Dear Customer,

Thank you for purchasing from Trivium Test Prep! We're honored to help you prepare for your big exam.

To show our appreciation, we're offering a **FREE *ASTB Essential Test Tips* DVD by Trivium Test Prep**. Our DVD includes 35 test preparation strategies that will make you successful on the ASTB exam. All we ask is that you email us your feedback and describe your experience with our product. Amazing, awful, or just so-so: we want to hear what you have to say!

To receive your **FREE *ASTB Essential Test Tips* DVD**, please email us at 5star@triviumtestprep.com. Include "Free 5 Star" in the subject line and the following information in your email:

1. The title of the product you purchased.

2. Your rating from 1 – 5 (with 5 being the best).

3. Your feedback about the product, including how our materials helped you meet your goals and ways in which we can improve our products.

4. Your full name and shipping address so we can send your **FREE *ASTB Essential Test Tips* DVD**.

If you have any questions or concerns please feel free to contact us directly at 5star@triviumtestprep.com. Thank you!

- **Trivium Test Prep Team**

ASTB Study Guide 2021–2022

Test Prep with Practice Questions for the Aviation Selection Test Battery Exam (ASTB-E)

Table of Contents

1. Introduction 6

   1.1 – Sections on the ASTB-E 6

   1.2 – Scoring on the ASTB-E 7

   1.3 – Additional Test Information 7

2. Mathematics Knowledge 9

   2.1 – Number Theory 9

   2.2 – Working with Fractions 15

   2.3 – Algebra 17

   2.4 – Geometry 21

3. Paragraph Comprehension 9

   3.1– Main Ideas 33

   3.2– Drawing Conclusions 35

   3.3– Stated Facts 35

   3.4– Mood and Tone 36

   3.5– Purpose 36

   3.6– Technique 37

   3.7– Sequence of Events 38

   3.8– Reworded Facts 39

4. Mechanical Comprehension 40

   4.1– Materials 40

   4.2– Fluid Dynamics 41

   4.3– Mechanical Motion 43

   4.4– Simple Machines 45

   4.5– Compound Machines 50

5. Aviation and Nautical Information 53

   5.1– Types of aviation and aircraft categories 53

   5.2– Aerodynamics forces 56

5.3– Additional aviation terms and definitions 60

5.4– General Shipboard Directions & Parts of a Vessel 66

5.5 -Basic Nautical Terms 67

6. Practice Test One 71

Paragraph Comprehension 71

Mathematics Knowledge 79

Mechanical Comprehension 86

Aviation and Nautical Information 94

Practice Test One Answer Key 101

7. Practice Test Two 105

Paragraph Comprehension 105

Mathematics Knowledge 115

Mechanical Comprehension 122

Aviation and Nautical Information 131

Practice Test Two Answer Key 138

Conclusion.. **Error! Bookmark not defined.**

1. Introduction

The ASTB-E, or "Aviation Selection Test Battery" is utilized by the Navy, Marine Corps, and Coast Guard to determine if candidates are qualified to selection for flight officer training programs. If going into the Navy, some portions of the test are used for general selection into officer candidate school, which is called the OAR or "Officer Aptitude Rating". The OAR score is comprised of only 3 of the 7 sections on the ASTB: Math Skills, Reading Comprehension, and Mechanical Comprehension. The test is administered through APEX or "Automated Pilot Examination" secure web-based testing platform. This platform was introduced December 9, 2013 and included some significant changes to the ASTB exam which will we review below.

1.1 – Sections on the ASTB-E

There are seven sections on the ASTB-E as follows:

1. Math Skills Test (MST)
2. Reading Comprehension Test (RCT)
3. Mechanical Comprehension Test (MCT)
4. Aviation and Nautical Information Test (ANIT)
5. Naval Aviation Trait Facet Inventory (NATFI)
6. Performance Based Measures Battery (PBM)
7. Biographical Inventory with Response Validation (BI-RV)

Of these seven sections, only the first four can truly be "studied" for. These sections are Math Skills, Reading Comprehension, Mechanical Comprehension, and Aviation & Nautical Information. These will be only sections covered in this book for the following two reasons: 1) the other sections cannot be studied for and 2) the information is closely guarded proprietary information, so is purposefully not available to anyone prior to taking the exam. We will provide as much information about these three sections below, so that you have at least some idea of what you might encounter.

The NATFI (Naval Aviation Trait Facet Inventory) is a questionnaire of personality traits which will help the military to determine potential career success. This information is proprietary and will not be released by the Navy. The only requirement is to answer the questions honestly, there is no way to "improve" or "study" for this section. You will be presented two statements and select the one that most applies to your personality.

Often, the statements have seemingly little to do with each other. For example, the statements might be "I often criticize my fellow employees" and "I do not like speaking in front of large groups".

The PBM (Performance Based Measures) section is a major change to the ASTB from the previous version. It includes the use of a joystick and throttle set as well as headphones to perform certain tasks. The general intention of this section is NOT to determine if you can already control an aircraft, but rather to determine your ability to perform tasks with other stimuli intended to distract you, as well as gauge your listening ability, and hand-eye coordination. According to the Navy, it is described as "A battery of processing speed, dexterity and divided-attention-driven tests measuring: Spatial orientation, Dichotic Listening, Ability to perform tracking tasks with stick-and-throttle set, and ability to perform several of these tasks at the same time". In short: it is a video game that tests your ability to multi-function while also seeing what your hand-eye coordination is like.

The BI-RV (Biographical Inventory with Response Validation) is designed to assess your "Previous experiences and background related to success in aviation". In short, it is a personality test of sorts and is not intended nor possible to study for. Like with the NATFI, simply answer the questions honestly and do not attempt to "tell them what they want to hear".

1.2 – Scoring on the ASTB-E

For those who only take the OAR portion of the exam will only receive one score, the "OAR Score" for Officer Candidate School. Those who take the entire test will receive three additional scores as listed below, which represent

- **Academic Qualifications Rating (AOR)** – Predicts Academic performance in Aviation Preflight Indoctrination (API) and primary phase ground school

- **Pilot Flight Aptitude Rating (PFAR)** – Predicts Primary flight performance for Student Naval Aviators (SNAs)

- **Flight Officer Aptitude Rating (FOFAR)** – Predicts Primary flight performance for Student Naval Flight Officers (SNFOs)

1.3 – Additional Test Information

Be sure that you visit www.med.navy.mil/sites/nmotc/nami/pages/astboverview.aspx (or simply Google "ASTB" and it will be the very first result) and review all the information on that page. This is the official source for information regarding the ASTB, so it is highly important you familiarize yourself with the content on that page and other sections of the website as well.

2. Mathematics Knowledge

The purpose of the **mathematics knowledge** section on the test is to make sure you fully understand the concepts that are important in high school mathematics courses. This includes information about basic operations, order of operations, algebra, and geometry. It also includes working with fractions, which can prove difficult for many people.

2.1 – Number Theory

Number theory is the study of the properties of whole numbers (0, 1, 2, …) and also integers, which are whole numbers plus their negative counterparts. Negative numbers can be thought of as inverses or opposites of whole numbers. Integers, like whole numbers, can be written without the use of a fractional part.

Prime Numbers

Prime numbers are numbers that have only two factors, 1 and itself. Examples would include 2, 3, 5, 7, 11, 13, 17, 19, and 23, as well as many others. When you are attempting to figure out if a number is a prime number or not, all you need to do is figure out whether other numbers, besides 1 and the number itself, will divide evenly into it.

Here are a couple of examples:

Is 66 a prime number?

66 is not a prime number. It can be divided by 2 and 33, 3 and 22, 6 and 11, as well as 1 and 66.

Is 21 a prime number?

21 is not a prime number, since 7 and 3 will divide into it, as well as 1 and 21.

It is important to note that prime numbers are typically odd, with the exception of the number 2. Even numbers clearly can be divided by 2, so even numbers larger than 2 will never be prime.

Mean (Average), Standard Deviation, Median, and Mode

You may be asked to find the **mean**, **standard deviation**, **median**, or **mode** of a set of numbers. The mean (average) of numbers is obtained by adding up all the numbers and then dividing by the number of numbers that you added up. The standard deviation is a measurement (which you probably won't have to compute!) of how far apart the numbers are from the mean or average. The median is obtained by ordering the numbers and picking the middle number, or averaging the two middle numbers. The mode is obtained by finding the number repeated the most number of times (if there is a number that repeats).

Multiples

Multiples of numbers are what results from multiplying whole numbers by other numbers. For example, multiples of 7 are 7, 14, 21, and so on.

Common multiples of two numbers are the numbers that are multiples of both. If you were looking at, for example, 4 and 8, then 16 would be a common multiple. 8 would also be a common multiple of the two numbers.

The least common multiple is the smallest common multiple that two given numbers share. The fastest way to find this is to just write out the first few multiples for both numbers that you have available and then figure out which one is the smallest. This is not a particularly difficult task, but you will have to understand how multiples work in order to do it properly. For example, the least common multiple of 4 and 8 is 8.

Factors

A **factor** is a number that goes evenly into another number with no remainder. So think of factors as all the numbers you can multiply together to get another number. Here is an example:

What are the factors of 24?

1 and 24, 2 and 12, 3 and 8, 4 and 6, since all of these numbers go into 24 exactly (without a remainder).

It is not necessary to write them like that, but it will help you keep them in mind if you keep the factors together with their counterparts. Another way to write these is 1, 2, 3, 4, 6, 8, 12, and 24.

If you want to figure out whether a number is a factor of another one or not, just divide the number by the potential factor and see if the result is a whole number. Every number will have at least two factors, 1 and the number itself. For example, the two factors of 2 are 1 and 2.

Common Factors

Numbers that are the factors of more than one whole number are known as **common factors**. For example, 6 would be a common factor of both 12 and 24 (because it can be multiplied by 2 to reach 12 and 4 to reach 24). The largest factor that goes into two numbers is called the greatest common factor.

Exponents

Exponents and exponential notation are used to help simply expressions, particularly when factors are repeated multiple times. Exponents are written as superscripts above the number that has the exponent. The number that has the exponent is called the base, so 8 is the base and 2 is the exponent in this example:

$$8 \times 8 = 8^2$$

Think of exponents as shorthand that is used to help keep the math straight and stop it from becoming too confusing. This can be seen below:

$$5 \times 5 \times 5 \times 5 \times 5 \times 5 = 5^6$$

Writing the number as an exponent makes it much easier to see what is happening and will simplify equations for you. Another way to say what is happening above is "five to the sixth power" or "five to the sixth". Here is another example where we are simplifying with an exponent:

$$2 + 2 \times 5 \times 5 \times 6 \times 7 + 8 = 2 + 2 \times 5^2 \times 6 \times 7 + 8$$

Does it simplify that equation a lot? Not in this case, but it does make it a little bit simpler to read.

Exponents are also used to denote cumbersome numbers in scientific notation; for example, $54000 = 5.4 \times 10^4$ and $.0043 = 4.3 \times 10^{-3}$.

Let's say a few words about fractional exponents and negative exponents. In an exponent that is a fraction, the number on the top acts just like an exponent, but the number on the bottom designates a "root" (see next section), which means a number would have to multiplied that many times to get to that number. For example, $8^{2/3} = (\sqrt[3]{8^2}) = (\sqrt[3]{8})^2 = 2 \times 2 = 4$. With negative exponents, you have to take the reciprocal of the base and make the exponent positive. For example, $2^{-3} = (\frac{1}{2})^3 = \frac{1}{8}$.

Also note that you can use exponents for questions dealing with combinations of letters or numbers. For example, if you were asked how many different numbers on a license plate there could be if the first three digits were letters, and the last 4 were numbers $0 - 9$, you'd have $26^3 \times 10^4$, since there are 3 places for 26 letters and 4 places for 10 numbers.

Square Roots

The term "**square root**" is used to describe a number that can be squared to equal the number provided.

The radical sign ($\sqrt{}$) is used to show square roots. For example, $\sqrt{9} = 3$, since $3^2 = 9$.

Some numbers will have very clean whole numbers for their roots. These are known as perfect squares. Here is a table that shows common perfect squares:

Number	Perfect Square	Square Root
1	1	$\sqrt{1}$
2	4	$\sqrt{4}$
3	9	$\sqrt{9}$
4	16	$\sqrt{16}$
5	25	$\sqrt{25}$
6	36	$\sqrt{36}$
7	49	$\sqrt{49}$
8	64	$\sqrt{64}$
9	81	$\sqrt{81}$
10	100	$\sqrt{100}$

Note that if we wanted the number that is multiplied 3 times to get a certain number, this is the cube root, so $\sqrt[3]{8} = 2$. We can use this same notation for 4th roots, and so on.

Order of Operations

The **order of operations** is the way that multiple operations need to be done in order to reach the correct answer. Some operations take precedence over others; mathematical operations don't also go from left to right, like reading does.

Here is the basic order of operations:

1. First take care of any operations that are within a grouping symbol such as parentheses () or brackets [].
2. Next handle the roots and the exponents.
3. Next handle the multiplication and division in the same order that they appear (left to right).
4. Finally, handle the addition and subtraction (again, moving from left to right).

As an example, consider the following:

$$\text{Solve: } 2 + 2 \times 2$$

If you ignore the order of operations, what do you get?

$$2 + 2 \times 2 = 4 \times 2 = 8$$

Now if you were to follow the order of operations, what happens?

$$2 + 2 \times 2 = 2 + 4 = 6$$

We get two different answers, but only the second is correct, since we need to perform multiplication before addition. It is important to eliminate any ambiguous statements in equations, because precision is key. That is why the order of operations is very important.

There is an acronym that can be used to help you remember the order of operations:

PEMDAS

Parentheses, Exponents, Multiplication/Division, Addition/Subtraction

If you are using PEMDAS, you need to remember that multiplication and division have to be completed as one step from left to right, and the same with addition and subtraction.

Working with Integers

Integers is a set that includes all whole numbers and the negatives (opposites) of those numbers as well. For example, integers are:

$$\dots -3, -2, -1, 0, 1, 2, 3 \dots$$

Think of *adding negative numbers* as the same as *subtracting positive numbers*. For example,

$$6 + -5 = 6 - 5 = 1$$

Addition and Subtraction with Positives and Negatives

There are two situations you will encounter when you have to add integers with negative sign(s). Are the numbers the same sign or are the numbers opposite signs? If the numbers are the same, then you can just add them like you normally would, and then add a negative sign to the answer if the two signs were negative to start out with. Here are a few example situations:

$$3 + 3 = 6$$
$$-3 + -3 = -6$$

So how do you handle a situation when the two numbers have different signs? Ignore the signs, subtract the smaller from the larger, and then use the sign of the greater of the two numbers. Here are a few examples:

$$3 + -4 = -1: \text{4 is greater than 3, so use the sign before the 4 (negative) in the}$$
answer

$$-5 + 4 = 1: \text{5 is greater than 4, so use sign before the 5 (positive) in the answer}$$

If you are subtracting, and have two negatives together, change them into one positive:

$$2 - -2 = 2 + 2 = 4$$

In all, the best way to handle subtraction with negative numbers is to just turn the problem into an addition problem.

You may also need to know that the **absolute value** (signified by $|\ \ |$) is the positive equivalent of positive and negative numbers. So $|-4| = 4$ and $|4| = 4$. So a number and the absolute value of its negative counterpart are equal.

Multiplication and Division with Positives and Negatives

Again, the best way to handle this is to ignore the signs and then multiply or divide like you normally would. To figure out what sign the final product will have, you simply have to figure out how many negatives are in the numbers you worked with. If the number of negatives is even, the result will be a positive number. If the number of negatives is odd, the result will be a negative number.

For example:

$$2 \times 2 \times -2 = -8: \text{one negative: odd number of negatives, so negative}$$

$$-2 \times -2 \times 2 = 8: \text{two negatives: even number of negatives, so positive}$$

$$-2 \times -2 \times -2 = -8: \text{three negatives: odd number of negatives, so negative}$$

Exponents of Negative Numbers

Exponents with negative numbers are relatively simple: If the number with the exponent (the base) is negative and the exponent is even, the result will be positive. If the number with the exponent is negative and the exponent is odd, the result will be negative. This is because, for example, $-4 \times -4 \times -4 \times -4 = 256$, but $-4 \times -4 \times -4 = -64$.

But we have to be careful with negative bases and even exponents. For even exponents, if the base is negative and in parentheses (or is a variable that you're putting in a number in for), the result is positive. For even exponents, if the negative sign is outside the parentheses, you have to raise the base to the exponent first, and then apply the negative (change the sign).

Here are some examples:

$$(-4)^2 = 16$$
$$-4^2 = -(4^2) = -16$$
$$(-3)^3 = -27$$
$$-3^3 = -(3^2) = -27$$

Evaluate x^2, where $x = -2$: $(-2)^2 = 4$

Evaluate $-x^4$, where $x = -2$: $-(-2)^4 = -16$

And again, remember that exponents are just another way of writing out multiplication.

2.2 – Working with Fractions

Check the arithmetic review section of this guide for information on how to convert fractions back and forth. This section will cover different types of fractions and how to perform operations on fractions.

Equivalent Fractions

Equivalent fractions are fractions that are equal. One of the most common things that you will do when you are working with fractions is to simplify them. Another way to state this is to "reduce" fractions. All this means is writing the fraction in the smallest equivalent fraction you can (smallest top and bottom). For example, $\frac{5}{10}$ and $\frac{2}{4}$ can both be simplified to $\frac{1}{2}$. So $\frac{5}{10}, \frac{2}{4}$, and $\frac{1}{2}$ are all equivalent fractions.

Here are some things to keep in mind when you are trying to simplify fractions:

- You need to find a number that can evenly divide into the top and the bottom number of the fraction that you are simplifying. After that, you can do the actual division.
- Once the division is finished, check to make sure your fraction cannot be further simplified. It is easy to make this mistake; even if you have found an equivalent fraction, it may be completely simplified, and your answer could be wrong.
- You can use simplification to reduce fractions to lower terms by dividing the top and bottom by the same number. You can also, perhaps more importantly, raise fractions to higher terms if you multiply both the top and the bottom numbers by the same number. This is very important in the addition and subtraction of fractions.

Here is an example of reducing a fraction:

$$\frac{6}{9} = \frac{2}{3}$$

The largest number you can divide into both of the numbers in the fraction (6 and 9) is 3. $\frac{6}{3} = 2$ and $\frac{9}{3} = 3$, giving the new fraction: $\frac{2}{3}$.

Here is an example of raising a fraction:

$$\frac{2}{4} = \frac{4}{8}$$

Simply multiply the 2 and the 4 each by 2 and you get the new equivalent fraction: $\frac{4}{8}$.

Addition and Subtraction

To add and subtract fractions, you need to understand two terms:

- **Numerator** – The number on the top of a fraction.
- **Denominator** – The number on the bottom of a fraction.

If you have two numbers that have the same denominator, you will have what is known as a common denominator. You can really only add or subtract fractions that have a common denominator, so if you do not have one, you need to make one, using equivalent fractions.

Here are the steps for adding and subtracting fractions:

1. If the fractions have a common denominator, then proceed as usual. If not, then reduce or raise one or both fractions until you have a common denominator.
2. Add or subtract the numerators as you would any number, ignoring the denominator.
3. Place the resulting sum (or difference) on top of the common denominator as the new numerator.
4. Simplify the new fraction as much as possible.

Step 1 is involved with coming up with what is known as the least common denominator. This is the smallest number that all fractions have as a common denominator. The process of doing this is the same as the process for finding the least common multiple.

You can turn mixed numbers into improper fractions before adding, for example:

$$2\frac{1}{2} + 3\frac{3}{4} = \frac{5}{2} + \frac{15}{4} = \frac{10}{4} + \frac{15}{4} = \frac{25}{4} = 6\frac{1}{4}$$

You can also add the whole number parts, then add the fractional parts, and then add the two together. This will save you a lot of trouble and extra steps. It is just as correct as any other method of solving the problem and, of course, remember that you are not being tested on how you did it, just that it was done. Here is the same problem:

$$2\frac{1}{2} + 3\frac{3}{4} = 2 + \frac{1}{2} + 3 + \frac{3}{4} = 2 + 3 + \frac{1}{2} + \frac{3}{4} = 2 + 3 + \frac{2}{4} + \frac{3}{4} = 5\frac{5}{4} = 6\frac{1}{4}$$

You do have to be careful subtracting mixed numbers, since you may have to borrow:

$$2\frac{1}{4} - 1\frac{1}{2} = 2\frac{1}{4} - 1\frac{2}{4} = 1\frac{5}{4} - 1\frac{2}{4} = \frac{3}{4}$$

A simpler way may be to turn mixed fractions into improper fractions:

$$2\frac{1}{4} - 1\frac{1}{2} = \frac{9}{4} - \frac{3}{2} = \frac{9}{4} - \frac{6}{4} = \frac{3}{4}$$

Multiplication and Division

Multiplication and division of fractions is actually simpler than adding or subtracting them. When you have to multiply fractions together, you'll first want to turn any mixed fractions into improper fractions. Then you just multiply the numerators to get the new numerator and then multiply the denominators to get the new denominator. Once that is done, you can go ahead and simplify.

For example:

$$2\frac{1}{5} \times \frac{3}{7} = \frac{11}{5} \times \frac{3}{7} = \frac{11 \times 3}{5 \times 7} = \frac{33}{35}$$

There is no way to simplify $\frac{33}{35}$, so this is the final answer.

Division is a little bit more complicated, but ultimately it is the same procedure. First, you have to find the reciprocal of the second fraction. A reciprocal is a fraction that is "flipped": its numerator and denominator are switched. Once that is done, you will multiply the fractions as usual.

Here is an example:

$$\frac{5}{6} \div \frac{2}{3} = \frac{5}{6} \times \frac{3}{2} = \frac{5 \times 3}{6 \times 2} = \frac{15}{12} = \frac{5}{4}$$

As you can see, the second fraction ($\frac{2}{3}$) simply flips to $\frac{3}{2}$. The common way this is explained is to "flip and multiply". That is as good an explanation as any, and is certainly easier to remember. Again, you are being tested on your ability to do the math here, not to know the jargon.

2.3 – Algebra

Algebra is a method of generalizing expressions involved in arithmetic. You will be able to explain how groups of things are handled all the time. This is useful for times when you have a certain function that you need to do over and over again. In algebra, you typically have numbers as well as symbols (usually letters) called "variables" that can be used to stand for certain numbers. Typically, variables are useful when dealing with word problems, since algebra makes it easier to solve for an "unknown."

Evaluating Numbers

Numbers that are assigned a definite value (like the number "1") are constants. When symbols (variables) are used to stand for numbers, they can typically take on any number. If you saw the equation: $2x = 6$, x would be the variable here, and in this case it would equal 3.

A few things to keep in mind:

- You can make a variable anything you want. X, y, Z, a, A, b, and so on are examples. They are usually italicized, to distinguish them from numbers.
- Both sides of the = sign are, obviously, =. So you can add or subtract or multiply or divide anything on both sides (constants or variables or both), as long as you do it to both sides. This is how you solve equations. With inequalities, however, you must change the sign if you multiply or divide by a negative number.
- Many times, you must distribute either variables or constants through to get rid of parentheses. For example, if you have $3(x - 9)$, you'll want "push through" the 3 to make it $3x - 27$.
- Once you have figured out what a variable is, plug it into the original equation to make sure everything is still equal.
- You may be asked to evaluate a function for a certain value in the variable. Just plug in that value everywhere the variable is. For example, the value of $f(3)$ in the function $f(x) = 3x + 2$ is $3(3) + 2 = 11$.

Equations

Equations are expressions that have an equal sign, such as $2 + 2 = 4$. Equations will usually have a variable, and will always be true or false. $2 + 2 = 1$ is false. $2 + 2 = 4$ is true. When you are solving for variables, there will typically only be one answer that will make the equation true. That is the number you must find.

Basically, to do this, you will just rewrite the equation in more and more simple terms until you have the solution to it. Ideally, you want this to be x (or whatever variable) = a number.

$$x = \#$$

Again, you can do anything to an equation as long as you do the same thing to both sides. This is how you solve equations.

Here is an example showing this:

$$3(x - 2) = -7 + 10$$

First, simplify anything you can on one side (the –7 and 10) and also get rid of any parentheses by "pushing through" (the "3" on the left hand side):

$$3x - 6 = 3$$

Next, add 6 to both sides to get the "$3x$" by itself:

$$3x - 6 + 6 = 3 + 6$$

$$3x = 9$$

Now, simplify this by dividing both sides of the equation by 3. Note: You have to divide the *entire* side by 3, not just one part of it:

$$\frac{3x}{3} = \frac{9}{3}$$

$$x = 3$$

Now, we have x all by itself on one side; the equation is now solved.

Note that if we have an **inequality** instead of an equation, we have to be careful. We solve an inequality the same way, but if we multiply or divide by a negative number, we have to switch the sign.

For example:

$$-3x - 2 \geq 4$$
$$-3x - 2 + 2 \geq 4 + 2$$
$$-3x \geq 6$$
$$\frac{-3x}{-3} \leq \frac{6}{-3}$$
$$x \leq -2$$

One more thing to mention here: If you are given an algebraic equation that is has 0 on one side and factors with variables, set each factor to 0 to solve for the variable. For example,

$$\text{Solve for } x: \quad (2x + 6)(3x - 15) = 0$$
$$2x + 6 = 0 \text{ and } 3x - 15 = 0; \quad x = -3, 5$$

An algebraic function like the one above is a polynomial of degree 2, which is a quadratic. To get the degree of a polynomial, add up all the exponents in each term, and the degree is the sum of exponents in the highest term. For example, for $4x^3y^5 + 8x^8y + 4x + 5$, the degree is 9, since in the second term, which has the largest sum of exponents, the sum of the exponents is $8 + 1 = 9$.

Word Problems

Word problems often utilize algebraic principles in their text. It is important to know how to properly assign a variable inside of a word problem. Pay attention to the words used: "x equals" or "a number equals", "x is less than", "2 is added to x", are common wordings. A lot of times, you can just "translate" the English right into the math; for example, "a number added to 5" would be "$x + 5$". Be careful though; "3 less than a number" would be "$x - 3$" (do the math with simple numbers to figure out wording).

If you are not given a specific variable but you need one, just call it whatever you want. "x" is the simplest variable you can use to do this, and is also one of the least confusing when you start working with more complex algebraic principles.

Here is a type of word problem you might encounter with ratios: A class of 140 has sophomores, juniors, and seniors in a ratio of 4:2:1. How many juniors are in the class? To solve this, you can set it up like this: $4x + 2x + 1x = 140$; $7x = 140$; $x = 20$. Since there are $2x$ juniors, there are $2 \times 20 = 40$ juniors in the class.

There is another type of algebra problem that you might encounter, and it involves "work". You can remember this equation: $\dfrac{\text{Time to do a job together}}{\text{Time to do a job alone}} + \dfrac{\text{Time to do a job together}}{\text{Time to do a job alone}} = 1$. For example, if we had a problem like "If Mark can do a job in 4 hours and John can do it in 3 hours, how long would it take for the two to do the job working together?", we'd have $\frac{x}{4} + \frac{x}{3} = 1$, to get $x = \frac{12}{7}$.

Also, always remember that Distance = Rate × Time.

Exponents – Multiplication

Multiplying variables with exponents is simple, as long as you have the same number with the exponent (the "base"). Just keep the same base and add the exponents together to get the new exponent. Keep in mind how exponents work as well; that is important.

Here is an example of exponents with variables:

$$x \times x \times x = x^3$$

Here is an example showing the multiplication of exponents; you can see why you add exponents:

$$x^2 \times x^3 = x^{2+3} = x^5, \text{ since } (x \times x) \times (x \times x \times x) = x^5$$

When raising something with an exponent in it to another exponent, you multiply exponents. And when dividing exponents, you do the opposite of addition, and subtract exponents with the same base. You may get a negative exponent; if you do, you can put it on the other side of the "division sign" and make it positive.

For example:

$$\frac{(2x^2y)^3}{x^4y^5} = \frac{8x^6y^3}{x^4y^5} = 8x^{6-4}y^{3-5} = 8x^2y^{-2} = \frac{8x^2}{y^2}$$

Polynomials

Polynomials are just a list of algebraic terms that can contain variables, constants, and exponents, but can never have any term that is divided by a variable.

To "combine like terms" you can add or subtract terms with the exact same variables. For example, $3x^2 + 2xy - 4 + 4x^2 - xy = 7x^2 + xy - 4$.

Note that if you have to multiply two two-term expressions to get a polynomial, use the FOIL (First, Outer, Inner, Last) method. For example,

$$(3x + 2)(x - 2) = (3x)(x) + (3x)(-2) + 2x - 4 = 3x^2 - 6x + 2x - 4 = 3x^2 - 4x - 4$$

If you have the same two-term expressions but with opposite signs (difference of squares), the middle terms (Outer and Inner) will cancel out:

$$(x + 2)(x - 2) = (x)(x) + (x)(-2) + 2x - 4 = x^2 - 4$$

Factoring

Factoring is the process of breaking one quantity down into the product of some other quantity (or quantities). When you learned to use distribution to multiply out variables ("push through"), you are learning to do the opposite of factoring. When you factor, you are removing parts of an expression in order to turn it into factors. Basically, you do this by removing the single largest common single term (monomial) that is a factor; this is the greatest common factor.

Here is an example of this:

$$\text{Factor the following: } 3x^2 - 9x$$

Basically, you will pull out the largest common denominator between the two of them. In this case, it is $3x$, since $3x$ goes into both $3x^2$ and $9x$. So you will be left with the following:

$$3x(x - 3)$$

To check this, "push through" the $3x$ to both the x and the 3, with a "–" sign in the middle; you get the original! It is also possible to do this with expressions that have more than two terms. Usually, these will be trinomials, with 3 terms. These will always end up being in the form of (x plus or minus something) times (x plus or minus something). What the second number is and what the sign is for the problem is determined by the original problem (we saw this above in the Exponents – Multiplication section).

Also, if you have a difference of squares, as we saw above, you can factor as the following:

$$(a^2 - b^2) = (a - b)(a - b)$$

Simplification

You can **simplify** algebraic expressions the exact same way that you would fractions by taking out common factors. They just cancel out. You may want to multiply everything out if you cannot find a factor and then simplify.

Here is an example:

$$\frac{(x+4)^2}{x+4} = \frac{(x+4)(x+4)}{x+4} = x + 4$$

The other thing to remember is if you have to add fractions with variables, you may have to find a common denominator. For example:

$$\frac{x - 2}{x} + \frac{x - 2}{x + 2} = \frac{(x - 2)(x + 2)}{x(x + 2)} + \frac{x(x - 2)}{x(x + 2)} = \frac{x^2 - 4 + x^2 - 2x}{x(x + 2)} = \frac{2x^2 - 2x - 4}{x(x + 2)}$$

2.4 – Geometry

The **geometry** section here is pretty straightforward. See the arithmetic reasoning portion of the guide for examples of perimeter and area. New information will be covered here.

Angles

Angles are typically measured in degrees. As an example, if you were to completely rotate around a circle a single time, you would have gone 360 degrees, since there are 360 degrees in a circle. Half a circle is 180 degrees, a quarter circle is 90 degrees, and so on. Degrees are used to talk about what fraction of a total rotation around a circle a certain angle represents.

Here is some terminology to keep in mind:

- **Acute angles** – Angles with a measurement of less than 90 degrees.
- **Right angles** – Angles with a measurement of exactly 90 degrees.
- **Obtuse angles** – Angles with a measurement of more than 90 degrees.
- **Complementary angles** – Two angles that add up to 90 degrees.
- **Supplementary angles** – Two angles that add up to 180 degrees.

Note that the sum of two angles that form a straight edge is 180 degrees. Note also that angles corresponding angles of parallel lines are equal.

For example:

_____

Triangles

Triangles are geometric figures that have three sides (which are straight). The most important thing you need to know about triangles is that the sum of the measurements of the angles always equals 180. This is important because it means that if you know two of them, you can very easily calculate the third simply by subtracting the first two from 180. There are three types of triangles that you need to know about:

- **Equilateral triangles** – These are triangles in which the three sides and three angles are the same measure. Each one of the angles is 60 degrees, since $3 \times 60° = 360°$.
- **Isosceles triangles** – These are triangles that have two sides of the same length. The two angles that are directly opposite the sides of the same length will be the same angle. If B was the third angle, then you could state that lines between A and B (AB) and between lines B and C (BC) are the same: AB = BC.
- **Right triangles** – These might be the most important. A right triangle is a triangle that has one side that equals 90 degrees. Two sides are legs and the third side, which is directly opposite the 90-degree angle, is the hypotenuse, and is the longest one of the sides.

With right triangles, you can always remember that the lengths of the sides are related by the following equation (the Pythagorean Theorem):

$$a^2 + b^2 = c^2$$

Remember that c is the hypotenuse, which is the side that is opposite the right angle. It is the longest of the sides.

The area of triangles is $\frac{bh}{2}$, where the base is perpendicular (form a right angle) to the base.

Also, with right triangle with two legs that are equal, the hypotenuse is always $\sqrt{2}$ times the value of a smaller side. For right triangles with 30-60-90 angles, the hypotenuse is always twice the smaller side (side across from the 30° angle), and the other leg (across from the 60° angle) is $\sqrt{3}$ times the smaller side.

Circles

A **circle**, as you probably are already aware, is a closed curve where every single point is the exact same distance from its center. If you draw a line from the outside of the circle to the fixed point in the center, you have the radius. If you draw a line from one side of the circle straight through to the other, passing through the center point, you have the diameter. A chord is a line from one point of the circle to another, but not necessarily a diameter. By the definition of a circle, all radii (plural of radius) are equal and all diameters are equal.

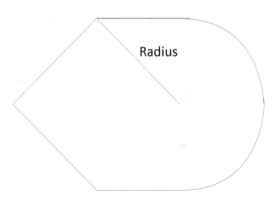

For a circle, remember:

$$\text{diameter} = 2 \times \text{radius}$$

You can use the radius to find out the circumference of a circle (how big it is around), by using the following formula:

C = circumference

r = radius

$$C = 2\pi r$$

Think of the circumference like the perimeter of the circle; if you were to take a piece of string all the way around a circle and measure it, this would be the circumference.

To find the area of a circle, use the following formula:

A = area

r = radius

$$A = \pi r^2$$

The area is the measurement of what's inside the circle and is written in square units.

The Coordinate System

The **coordinate system** or, sometimes, the Cartesian coordinate system, is a method of locating and describing points on a two-dimensional plane; It is a reference system. The plane is two number lines that have been laid out perpendicular to each other, with the point that they cross being origin (0, 0). The origin is the point "0" for both the x (horizontal) and y (vertical) axes. Positive and negative integers are both represented in this system.

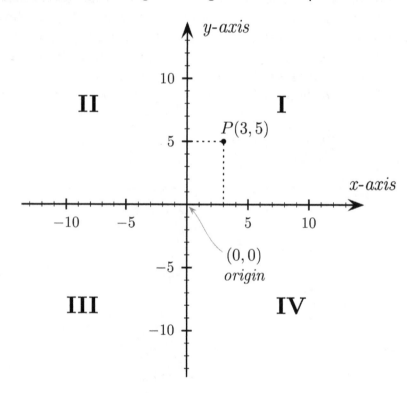

In the image above, each small tick on the line is equal to one. The larger ticks represent multiples of 5. A point is also depicted, *P*, which shows how things are placed onto the coordinate system. Again, the horizontal line on the coordinate plane is called the *x*-axis, and the vertical line on the coordinate plane called the *y*-axis. The points, when described, are described in reference to where they lie on that plane.

Here is an example that is the point shown above:

$$(3, 5)$$

The first number, 3, is the x-axis. The second, 5, is the y-axis. So this point is at position 3 of the x-axis (go over 3 units to the right) and position 5 of the y-axis (go up 5 units). Note that for negative x values, we go to the left that many units, and for negative y values, we go down.

A way to simplify the way these points work is to say:

$$(x, y)$$

Slope

The **slope** is the steepness of a given line. When you look on the coordinate plane, if you draw a line between two points, you will get the slope. One of the main uses of a slope is to signify a rate; it measures how much a certain thing goes up for every unit it goes over.

Here is the way to find slope:

Point A: (x_1, y_1)

Point B: (x_2, y_2)

$$\text{Slope} = \frac{(y_2 - y_1)}{(x_2 - x_1)}$$

In plain English, you will take the difference between the y coordinates and divide them by the difference between the x coordinates. Remember: y is vertical and x is horizontal.

Here is an example:

Find the slope of a line with that goes through the following points: $(9, 3), (2, 12)$

First, set the problem up (always do the subtractions from the same point):

$$\frac{12 - 3}{2 - 9}$$

Next, solve the differences:

$$\frac{9}{-7}$$

So the slope of the line that goes through those two points is $-\frac{9}{7}$. You can solve this for a decimal, but there is no need to do that.

Some things to remember:

- If the slope is positive, the line is going up as it goes right.
- If the slope is negative, the line is going down as it goes right.
- The larger the absolute value (positive value) of the slope, the steeper the line.
- If a line is horizontal, its slope is 0; if a line is vertical, its slope is undefined.
- The formula for a line is $y = mx + b$, where m is the slope and b is the y-intercept (where the line crosses the y-axis).

- If two lines are parallel, they have the same slope. If they are perpendicular, they have negative reciprocal slopes.
- If two lines are intersection, the *x* and *y* values work in both equations; in other words, if you were to plug in the *x* and *y* values, both equations would be true. This is how you "solve" a system of equations.

2.5 – Tips

Here are some tips to help you make it through the **mathematics knowledge** section of the ASVAB:

- Remember to utilize PEMDAS and the order of operations when you are working through problems.
- The more you practice, the easier the problems will be. There are a lot of internet sites with math problems.
- Be careful with the answers. The test will often provide common mistakes answers among the correct answer.
- Since you will not have access to a calculator, you will need to round π. 3.14 or $\frac{22}{7}$ are the most common ways to do this. Sometimes you may be asked to simply include it in your answer without actually utilizing the digits in your calculations at all.
- Don't mix up the perimeter and area formulas.
- One way to get good at algebra relatively quickly is to set up all of your problems, even simple ones, as algebra problems. Remember, you can simply create a variable and stick it on one side of the equation to solve for it. For example, "3 times a number added to 10 is 16" becomes "$3x + 10 = 16$". Translate almost word-for-word from English to math, and then get *x* by subtracting 10 from each side, and then diving by 3.
- Keep in mind that, unlike many tests you probably remember taking in high school, you are not being tested on your ability to write out how you solved the problem. There are many correct ways to solve mathematical problems and, as long as you come to the right answer in the end, it does not matter how you solved it. Nobody will be coming behind you and checking your scratch paper to see what you did (unless they think you are cheating, but that is a whole other ball of wax).
- If you can't solve the problem directly, trying plugging in the answers to see if you can figure out which one works.
- Pay close attention to the positive and negative signs in the work that you are doing. This is extremely important because, again, they will likely throw the correct answers out there as one of the choices but with the wrong sign.
- Always make sure the fractions that you are working with are simplified when you finish with them. Unless otherwise stated, the test answers will usually want the most simplified version of the fraction.

- Make sure you go step by step through each question. Don't skip steps or combine steps. Doing either could lead to an issue where something is accidentally missed.
- It might help you to change even the normal expressions into algebra. Often, understanding what you are being asked to do and knowing how to handle certain problems is only made easier when you are using algebra to handle it.
- Draw pictures on geometry problems.

3. Paragraph Comprehension

The purpose of the paragraph comprehension section of the ASTB is to figure out how well you understand the things that you read. It also measures the level of your ability to retain information that you have read in passages. This is one of the 4 subtests on the ASTB which has its score counted toward your AFQB score, so scoring a high number on this subtest is important to your future military career. There are 15 questions on this test which are based on either 15 distinct passages or a number of passages less than 15. Each passage will have a set of questions that is associated with it and you will generally have to pick the answer that best answers a question or fills in a statement to make it complete.

There are two skills which are used to help you understand the things that you read. One of them is the ability to understand what the passage you have read actually says. This is the literal reading of the passage. Some of the questions found on the test are going to ask you to determine what a passage means or to paraphrase something which has been said. To understand a paraphrase, you will have to understand what the original passage means, obviously. This also means you need to understand words in the context of the passage.

The second skill you need is the ability to analyze the things that you read. This means you will have to go a bit deeper than the literal interpretation of the passage. You will be asked, at times, to draw conclusions based on information contained within the passage itself. This will often require you to figure out things which are stated indirectly (or not at all) in the content of the passage. Sometimes you will be asked about the tone of the passage or the mood that it evokes.

There are a few types of questions that you will likely encounter in this section of the test:

Main Idea Questions

This type of question wants you to give a general statement about what the paragraph you have read means.

Here is an example of this type of question:

> The economy is making a slow comeback. The housing boom of the 90s is not back, but it should be clear that the economy is improving from where it was just a few years ago.

> This is even in the face of fruit markets which have been slowing down, causing trouble for bankers and others as well.

What is the main idea of the prompt listed above?

- A) The economy is not doing well.
- B) The economy is on its way back.
- C) Bankers are losing money.
- D) The apple market isn't good.

The answer here is B. The thesis statement in the first sentence says the economy is on an upswing. Bankers may be losing money, the apple market (and other fruit markets) may not be doing well, but the economy in general is improving, making B the best choice in this situation.

Sequence of Events Questions

These types of questions are asking about the order that events occur in the passage. Here is an example of a sequence of events type of question:

> The walls were the first thing to fall. Once they had fallen, ranks quickly began to break and the soldiers prepared for a full retreat. Finally, there was the castle itself, which was the last to fall.

In what order did things happen?

- A) Castle fell, then retreat, then the walls fell
- B) Retreat, castle fell, walls fell
- C) Walls fell, retreat, castle fell
- D) Walls and castle fell followed by retreat

The answer is C. The events took place in a clear order. First the walls, then the retreat, then the castle fell.

Rewording of Facts Questions

These types of questions will ask about facts in the text, but the answers will not have the exact same wording as the passage does. Instead, they will mean the same thing but the wording will be different.

Here is an example of a reworded fact type of question:

> Apple sales at the local market have been booming. 300 Granny Smith apples, 200 Fuji apples, and 150 Pink Lady apples have been sold in the last week alone. Those numbers are huge

compared to what they were before the latest health food craze hit this part of the state. It is very good for apple farmers as well.

Which of the following is true?

- A) More Fuji apples were sold than anything.
- B) More Pink Lady apples were sold than Fuji apples.
- C) Granny Smith apples were the top seller last week.
- D) People hate Granny Smith apples.

The answer is C. It is clear that they sold the most. This is a simple comparison problem, even without doing any math at all you can see that Granny Smith apples were the bestselling type of apple last week, which is another way of stating what is being said in the prompt.

Stated Facts Questions

This type of question primarily relies on facts which are stated in the passage. You should avoid using any outside information for these questions. In addition, your answer will need to say everything that is in the passage with regard to the question itself. Often, you will want to find an answer that uses the exact wording that you found in the passage.

Here is an example of a stated fact type of question:

Ten boys went to the church function, along with five girls, six adults, and no children under two years old.

How many children under two years old went to the church function?

- A) ten
- B) two
- C) three
- D) none

The correct answer here is D. No children under two years old went to the church function.

Mood and Tone Questions

Mood and tone questions are about the emotions that are suggested by the content that you have read.

Here is an example of a mood and tone question:

It was a beautiful day. The sun was shining and everything was going great. Blue skies and white clouds were everywhere and, best yet, my little cousin and I were at the park together eating cotton candy!

What emotions does this prompt elicit in the reader?

A) happiness

B) sadness

C) anger

D) loneliness

It is pretty clear that A, happiness, is the correct answer in this situation. Blue skies, cotton candy, the park? What could be happier than that?

Purpose Questions

This type of question concerns itself with the purpose of the passage. Here is an example of a purpose type of question:

Welcome to the manual for your new blender! Here are a few things you need to know to get started using it! Plug in the AC adapter into the nearest wall outlet and then press the power button to turn the blender on.

What is the purpose of the above prompt?

A) to explain the use of the new blender

B) to say what the blender is for

C) to get someone to buy the blender

D) to blend something

A. Obviously. This is an easy one. Typically, though, this type of question is going to be straightforward and relatively easy to answer.

Technique Questions

Technique questions want you to identify techniques that form the basis of the structure of the passage you have read. Here is an example of a question of this type:

Her eyes were the moon reflected on a still ocean.

What technique was used in the above prompt?

    A) simile

    B) metaphor

    C) onomatopoeia

    D) exaggeration

The answer is B. That is the best answer. It is not a simile because "like" or "as" are not used.

Questions about Conclusions

Conclusions questions are about indirect conclusions that you can infer from the text you have read. Here is an example:

> The church is running out of money. Unless donations begin to come up and the rise of atheism as a state religion is stemmed, it will be extremely difficult to continue most of the community programs which have evolved over the last fifty years.

> Which of the following is the best conclusion that you can draw based on the text in the prompt above?

>   A) less help can be given to the community because of lack of funds

>   B) churches are doing great

>   C) atheism is stealing money from the church

>   D) the church has only been around for fifty years

The answer is A. The entire purpose of the prompt is talking about the church and their lack of funding. It is easy to draw the conclusion spoken about in A, because it is basically stated.

On the following page is a table outlining the line scores that utilize the paragraph comprehension subtest score for each branch of the military.

Table 3.1. Subtest scores

Branch	Line Score
Army	Clerical, General Technical, Skilled Technical, Operators and Food, Surveillance and Communications
Marines	General Technical
Navy/Coast Guard	Administrative, Health, Nuclear, General Technical
Air Force	Administrative and General

The general method of study for the paragraph comprehension portion of the test involves studying the individual type of questions that you will encounter in it. Obviously that sounds simpler than it actually is, but this section is, as the word comprehension, a matter of knowing what to prepare for rather than cramming. This section is akin to a "know it or don't know it" type of situation. The best thing to do is know the types of questions, learn the general tips, take practice questions and tests, and read voraciously. Doing those things will give you the best foundation for this subtest.

3.1– Main Ideas

The main idea section concerns itself with exactly what you think: the main idea. Main ideas are going to be general statements that sum up what a given passage is about. Information about the paragraph itself is usually specific and provides support for the main idea, which is often outlined in the very first sentence. Sometimes the main idea is referred to as a thesis statement.

The main idea is sometimes stated directly, but not always. If it is stated, it might be referred to as the topic sentence. Usually happening right at the beginning of a paragraph. Usually, the main idea or the topic sentence will not be found in the middle or the end of a passage, but it can be.

Usually, when you are asked to talk about the main idea, the right answer might be worded differently than the way it is stated in the paragraph. If the writer has chosen to not directly state the main idea, you need to figure out what it is by reviewing all of the information in the passage and determining what general point is being made. This is known as "inferring" the main idea.

The first thing you will want to do when you are trying to come up with the main idea for a given prompt is to look at the very first and the very last sentences of the passage. This does *not* mean you should neglect to read the rest of the passage, but those two sentences are generally the most important. Take a look at the following prompt, for example:

> Local farmers are having trouble watering their crops due to the drought. Since last year, over ten thousand gallons of water have evaporated from the local fields. Combined with the lack of rain, local crops are dying off. Farmers might have reduced crop yields as a result.

What would be the main idea here? The main idea is right there in the first sentence. "Local farmers are having trouble watering their crops due to the drought." The rest of the paragraph is only supporting evidence for that main point. You should keep in mind, however, that the main idea is not always going to be the one in the first sentence. Sometimes a paragraph is going to build up the main idea before stating it. Take a look at the following prompt for an example of this:

> Local gardens are beginning to blossom. Bees are buzzing near the flowers and flying around the trees. Kids are beginning to come outside instead of staying inside out of the cold. The sun is warming everything up. Spring is here!

The main idea in this case is stated in the final sentence, "spring is here". The rest of this paragraph is being used in order to provide some context and supporting evidence for that main idea.

Note: The main idea, again, is not always going to be stated outright. Sometimes it is going to be indirect or implied. One of the answers, however, should obviously be talking about the main idea.

Writers do not always talk about only one specific point, however, so you need to be prepared to identify sub-points in your paragraph. Details are often included which will support the main idea and they will usually be helping you to prove whatever point the main idea is stating.

If you are having trouble coming up with the main idea, you might try attempting to paraphrase the prompt that you are reading. You can do that without even putting a lot of effort into it, simply do it in your head while you read. If you begin doing this with the things that you read now, you will find yourself improving very quickly.

3.2– Drawing Conclusions

These types of questions want you to draw conclusions based on what is in the passage. Often, the writer will not directly state the conclusions that you are meant to draw, but they will be indirectly stated. Usually, they are obvious. Take the pieces of information which are in the passage and then put them together to see what sorts of things are implied. The passage usually will not give you an answer to your question directly and the things which are stated directly in the passage are not conclusions. The conclusion is based on the relationships between the information you have been presented.

Take the following prompt, for example:

> Most burglaries that occur in residential homes are because people neglected to lock their house up properly when they leave. The resulting crimes, thus, are crimes of opportunity.

What sorts of conclusions can you draw here? Well, there are a few, not all of them are correct, however. Here are some of the possible conclusions you could come up with:

- Some crimes only occur because someone was neglectful of safety.
- Preventing opportunity will prevent crime.
- Most burglaries are caused by residential homeowners.

The last, obviously, is likely a bad conclusion to draw. It is, however, one that you could come up with based on the information contained in the prompt itself.

3.3– Stated Facts

These questions are easily the simplest questions on this subtest. All they do is ask you for a fact which was stated in the passage. The wording will be the same. The exact same statement from the answer will be seen in the passage. Do not be tempted to use outside information which is not located inside of the text. The only information that you will be getting here is going to be inside the passage. Again: The information is ONLY about what is contained in the passage and nothing else.

Take the following passage, for example:

> Fuji apples were originally created by gardeners working in Japan in the 1930s. They are a type of hybrid apple which resulted from a combination of Red Delicious apples and Virginia Ralls Genet apples. They are large, round, and very sweet (especially when compared with some other types of apples).

Take a moment to look over this and find some of the stated facts that are in this paragraph. Once you have done that, take a crack at the following question:

1. The Fuji apple is an apple that is
    a. large, round, and very sweet
    b. large, round, and yellow
    c. a non-hybrid apple
    d. grown only in Japan

The answer here is A. That is the only fact that is stated directly. It is stated in the very last sentence of the paragraph. What are some other facts that are in this paragraph?

- Fuji apples are a hybrid of Red Delicious and Virginia Ralls Genet
- Fuji apples are sweet when compared to other apples
- Fuji apples originated in Japan
- Fuji apples were originally created in the 1930s

3.4– Mood and Tone

The mood and the tone of a given passage are a representation of the emotions that the content is trying to elicit in the reader. When you are faced with these types of questions, you will want to think about the type of language that is being used. Are they happy? Are they sad? You can usually tell immediately. If the skies are said to be dark and it is raining, the mood is likely sad or depressed. If the sun is out and the sky is bright, the mood will likely be happy.

Think about how you might feel if you were suddenly dropped into the world of the passage. Whatever emotions you would likely be feeling at that time are the ones you will probably be feeling in the context of the passage itself.

3.5– Purpose

Questions about purpose will try and get at what the passage is intended for. What it is aiming to accomplish. Some writings are meant to provide the reader with information. Some are meant to provide instructions on how to do something. Some are persuasive and try to convince the person reading it of something. The purpose would be what the writing wants to do.

When trying to figure out what a passage is purporting to do, you should look at how the various sentences within it connect and relate with one another. If the passage is mostly evidence for the thesis statement, it is likely an argumentative passage. You should readily be able to tell if it is instructional or if it is meant to tell a story. You can practice this by doing it for each paragraph of the things that you read.

The conclusions that you draw about the meaning of a given prompt is what allows you to get to new ideas which are not directly stated in the text. All of the information which is being given to you by the author should be analyzed in order to find inferences that may be present in the text. You can use the example prompt from earlier in order to illustrate this idea:

> Local farmers are having trouble watering their crops due to the drought. Since last year, over ten thousand gallons of water have evaporated from the local fields. Combined with the lack of rain, local crops are dying off. Farmers might have reduced crop yields as a result.

One thing you could infer from this text, for instance, is that the additional of rainfall would correct the problem that the farmers are having with their crops. The crops are dying because of the lack of water and the lack of rain. The addition of water/rain would fix this problem.

Clearly this is not directly stated by the author, but all of the information required to come to that conclusion is right there in the text.

What are some other things that you might be able to infer from this passage? Here is a brief list of a couple:

- The drought probably began last year.
- The issue is a combination of heat and lack of rain ("evaporated" is the keyword).

3.6– Technique

Writing is always organized into some sort of structure. Various techniques are used to do this, and the technique questions on the ASTB concern themselves with those techniques. They might ask you how a passage is structured. They might ask about keywords. Often, there are some tells that you can use to try and determine what sort of passage you are reading and these same words can be used to help determine the sequence of events and the purpose of the passage as well.

Words are the key to figuring out the technique being used. Here are some things to keep in mind:

- Narrative technique uses words like "first", "soon", "then", "next", or might provide you with brief time frames of when events are happening.

- Descriptive technique will use spatial descriptions of what is happening and might utilize the senses (sight, sound, taste, touch, smell).

- Look for words that relate things to each other in space like "on", "next to", "beside", "under", etc.

- Comparison is used as a technique with words like "similarly", "like, "same", etc.

- Contrast can also be done, using words like "as opposed to", "on the other hand", "but", etc.

- If information is presented about why things are happening, this can be the technique of cause and effect. Look for things like "since", "because", "resulting in", "so", etc.

In this section, you might also encounter some literary techniques. Some that you have heard of, some that you may not have heard of. Here is a brief rundown of a few of these types of techniques that you can learn:

- **Simile** – A simile is a technique that is used to compare things with the usage of some sort of connecting word (than, so, as, like, etc.).

- **Metaphor** – This is a technique which is meant to compare unrelated things through the use of rhetorical effect.

- **Ellipsis** – The deliberate omission of certain words.

- **Elision** – Omitting letters in speech. This is what leads to the colloquial speech that many people use when texting or chatting online.

- **Hyperbole** – A form of exaggeration.

- **Onomatopoeia** – Using a word to imitate a real sound (such as "boom" for an explosion).

Obviously there are many techniques, but this should give you a good enough basis for what you are likely to find on the ASTB.

3.7– Sequence of Events

Questions about the sequence of events are exactly how they sound. They are asking about what order the events of the prompt are occurring in. You will want to spend your time looking at the prompt and picking out words that talk about time. These could be words such as "before," "then," "next," "finally," etc. These are the types of words which indicate what events happened and when they happened. This is a relatively simple thing to do and these types of questions are usually not too complicated.

3.8– Reworded Facts

Reworded facts are pretty easy to understand. All you need to do is look for facts that have been stated in the prompt to answer the questions. Usually, you will have to pick an answer which means the exact same thing as something which has been stated in the passage itself, though the words will not always be the same.

4. Mechanical Comprehension

The mechanical comprehension subtest is meant to help determine how well you understand the basics about physics and forces. This section includes things such as work, pressure, hydraulics, and mechanical advantage. Sometimes, the questions you are asked will include an image that you will need to use to answer.

The mechanical comprehension subtest on the ASTB is an overview of basic physics, how machines work, and how you can use mechanics to your own advantage. This section is not too complicated and does not go too in-depth into the physics, but it is a section which is important to understand for a number of subspecialties. It is not one of the core tests which goes into calculating your AFQT score.

This section of the ASTB consists of 25 questions that need to be answered within 19 minutes.

4.1– Materials

Materials are all of the things which are used for building, constructing things, and work. Some of these are better for specific uses than others. Wood is good for building small to medium sized structures and for quick projects. Metal is good for precision projects, things that need to have rigorous standards, and for larger structures. Small containers which are meant to hold things might be made of cardboard, paper, or something similar.

Here are some examples of common materials:

- Steel
- Wood
- Iron
- Glass
- Cardboard
- Paper
- Wool
- Cotton

Properties

Different materials have different properties and characteristics. These are important to understand if you want to select the right materials for the right job.

Here are some of the most important material properties:

- **Weight** – The force that is on an object due to gravity. How much force is going to be required to move the object.

- **Density** – Density is a measure of mass per unit of volume. Basically, how much "stuff" is inside something.

- **Strength** – How well the object can maintain the shape that it has when it is being subjected to pressures and forces from the outside.

- **Contraction** – How much the object will shrink when subjected to certain temperatures.

- **Expansion** – How much the object will enlarge when subjected to certain temperatures.

- **Absorption** – A measure of how well a material can pick up and hold liquid that contacts it.

- **Center of gravity** – This is the point of the object where it can be balanced (equal force on all sides).

Structural Support

Structural support is a concept which combines many of the material properties that were discussed in the previous section. It is, generally, a way to take a specific amount of materials and use it in such a way that it is able to support a given amount of weight. Consider buildings, tables, and other common creations. All of these have to hold up a specific amount of weight, but the amount that they can hold up depends on their specific properties.

4.2– Fluid Dynamics

Solids and liquids behave in very different ways. This section will explain what differences exist. *Viscosity* is a term which is utilized to describe how easily a fluid is able to flow. This is a term which is particularly important when it comes to engines. Another term which is important to understand is *compressibility*. This is one of the most important concepts in fluid dynamics.

Solids can be compressed with relative ease. Liquids, however, cannot be. The pressure of a liquid will spread out amongst the entirety of the liquid and become equal at all points.

The summary of the main points in the study of hydraulics, thus, would be that liquids are very difficult to compress and that pressure is equal throughout a liquid. Pressure, of course, is defined as the force per unit area. Thus, since the pressure is equal everywhere, if you have a small opening at one end of a container, the pressure will be equal to a large opening at the other. So you can use a small force to push on the smaller end and have a large effect on the larger opening.

Figure 4.1. Fluid dynamics

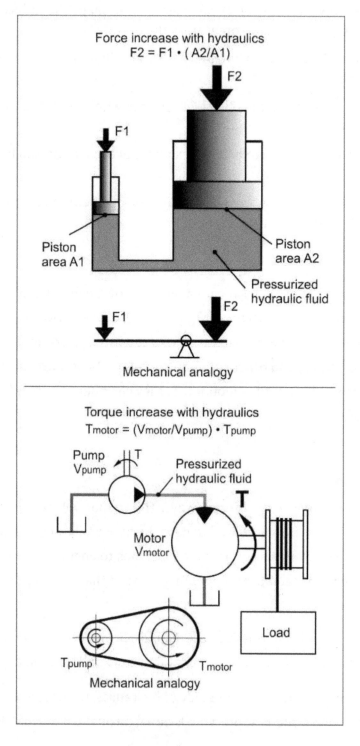

4.3– Mechanical Motion

Figure 4.2. Common hydraulic system

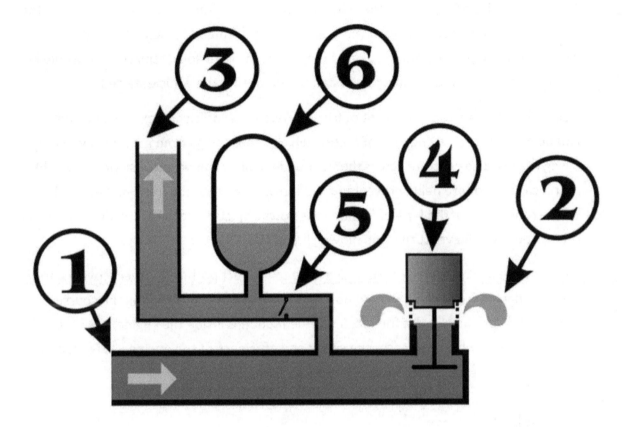

Mechanical motion is a fancy term for just motion. This is the study of how objects move. There are a few terms you will have to understand before getting started with this, some of which have already been covered in this guide.

Here is a brief refresher:

- **Speed** – the total distance traveled divided by the total time required to travel
- **Velocity** – the total displacement divided by the time in which the displacement has taken place.
- **Acceleration** – This is the change in speed divided by the time it takes for the change in speed to occur.

You may be having trouble understanding the difference here, so some clarification may be required. Consider the following scenario:

A car drives around a circular track that has a length of 2 miles. The car drives around the track 3 times in 3 minutes. How fast is the car going?

Well, a total of 6 miles was traveled. 6 miles in 3 minutes is 2 miles per minute. 2 x 60 = 120 or, 120 miles per hour. But the velocity is zero. Why is the velocity zero? Because the car ended exactly where it began. There was no displacement because the track is a circle. This is the primary difference and is a source of confusion. Displacement would be the distance between the ending point and the point that the vehicle started.

Next, you will come to the concept of friction. Two types of friction exist: static and kinetic. Static friction is the type of friction which keeps things from moving. If you are trying to push a heavy crate across the floor and it will not move because of the weight that it carries, you are being prevented from moving due to static friction. Kinetic friction, on the other hand, is the type of friction that slows objects which are already moving. This is why your car will eventually stop moving if you take your foot off the gas.

Engines have a lot of moving parts which have to interact both with other moving parts and with parts of the engine that do not move. The moving parts, during the course of their motion, product kinetic friction. Since the friction is inside the engine, it is called internal friction, which decreases the speed and efficiency of the engine. Oil is used to lubricate engine parts and to help overcome this type of friction.

Centrifugal Force

Most people are familiar with what a centrifuge is. If you aren't, then know that it is a machine which has a design that allows it to spin quickly to separate liquids and solids from each other that have been in solution. The reason this works is relatively simple: the machine is spinning but the liquids inside are trying to continue going in a straight line and, thus, are able to separate based on their relative weights.

Figure 4.3. Centrifuge

The easiest way to think about this is when you are in a car. If you were to take a fast right turn in a vehicle, what would happen? Your body would feel like it was being pulled to the left. In truth, the car is pulling to the right and your body is just trying to maintain the direction that it was already going (in a straight line).

4.4– Simple Machines

Simple machines are utilized in a variety of ways almost universally every single day. These machines are, in truth, something that most people would not even consider machines. To understand how these work, you need to understand the concept of mechanical advantage. *Mechanical advantage* is a measure of how much a job is being made easier by the assistance of a simple machine.

Here is the formula for calculating mechanical advantage:

- R = the distance from the applied force to the pivot point
- X = the distance from the pivot point to the magnified force
- mechanical advantage = R/X

The first kind of simple machine that you need to understand is the lever. A lever is also referred to as a lever arm. This is going to be a rigid (non-flexible) object which is pivoting around a point. The idea being that force which is applied on one end of the lever will be magnified at the other end.

Figure 4.4. Lever

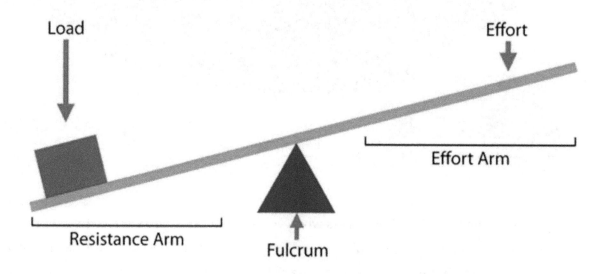

In the image above, when you apply force to the effort arm, the lever will bend about the fulcrum and apply a force to the resistance arm which will be magnified by an amount that can be determined by using the formula for mechanical advantage.

The next type of simple machine that you need to understand is an inclined plane. This is simply a plan which can be used to help you move something from one height to a different height.

Usually, these are used to help move heavy boxes or objects from lower points to higher points. Think about this as it is in the real world: a ramp. Pushing a box up a ramp to a height of five feet is a lot easier than picking the box up and lifting it five feet.

Figure 4.5. Inclined plane

THE INCLINED PLANE

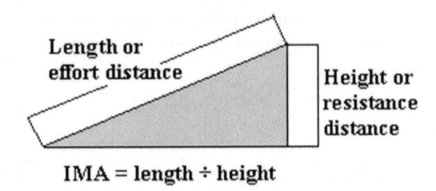

The next type of simple machine is a screw. These are typically used to hold things together, often two pieces of wood or metal. The screw has threads which will hold fast to the material and prevent it from being pulled back out easily.

Figure 4.7. Screws

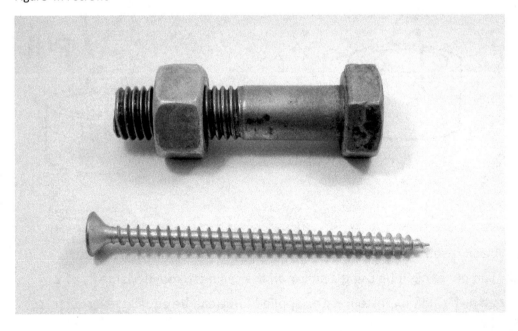

When looking at the screw in the image above, think about what is happening when it is going into a material. The threads are removing small bits of material, but only enough to fit itself inside. Thus, it sits snugly inside the material.

The next kind of simple machine is a pulley. This is a little bit more complex than the other simple machines that have already been covered. This type of machine has many uses, one of which is helping to lift objects from the ground when used along with a piece of rope.

Figure 4.8. Pulley

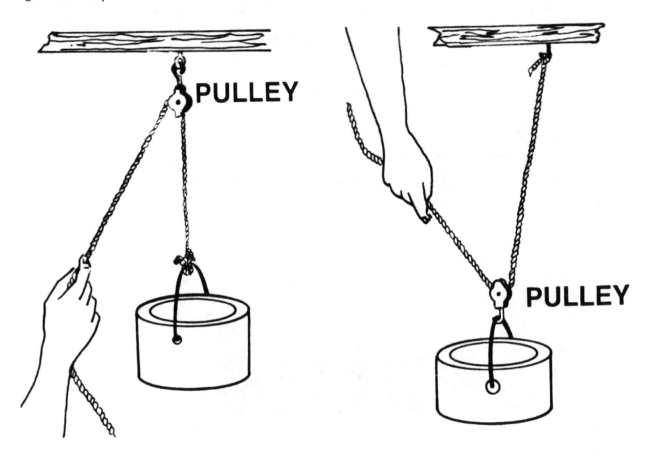

Pulleys are typically used to pull something from one point to a point at a different height easily. Someone might be using a pulley on the ceiling to move a large box from the floor up to a high shelf, for instance. The applied force can be equal to exerted force in some situations.

Depending on the exact way that the pulley is being used, the force that you are applying to the pulley can be greatly increased.

The next type of simple machine is a wedge, which is typically utilized to split objects and separate them from each other. A crowbar might be an example of this (and an example of a lever). Another might be a hatchet or an ax. A nail is an example as well.

Figure 4.9. Wedge

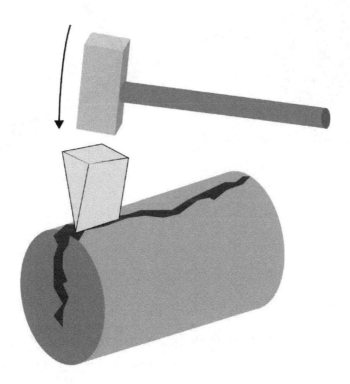

Where the wedge is very thin, it can be inserted and force can be applied to get it to go inside of the object which is to be separated. Once that happens, the width of the wedge increases so that the farther it goes into the object, the more it pushes the object apart. In the image above, you can see how this would work.

The next type of simple machine is the wheel and axle. When force is applied to the axle through the turning of the wheel, the axle will transfer the force. The most common example of this is the faucet used to get water outside of your home (or the steering wheel on your car).

Figure 4.10. Wheel and axle

When you turn the steering wheel, the axle that is attached to it will turn the gear on the other end, which will, in turn, move the wheels in the directions you want them to go. This is the basis for the steering in vehicles, among many other things.

4.5– Compound Machines

Compound machines are machines which have moving parts and more than one component, usually. These are usually utilized for the same general reasons as simple machines would be. They are meant to allow a mechanical advantage for completing a specific task.

A cam is an example of a compound machine. The cam is going be turned by a piston, thus converting the linear motion of the piston into a circular motion. As the rod turns, it turns the ring which is attached to it. This is the method by which many types of devices work, including combustion engines and certain types of pumps.

Another type of compound machine would be a system of gears. One gear will turn and its teeth will then turn a second gear. Small gears will usually have fewer teeth than large gears, and the number of rotations that each gear goes through in the system will change. The mechanical advantage in this situation is defined by how many teeth the gears have. Divide the number of teeth on the large gear by the number of teeth on the small gear and you will have your mechanical advantage. Gear systems are commonly used in vehicles inside of transmissions.

The next type of compound machine is a crank, which is a rod that has a variable radius that has a chain wrapping around the portion of the rod with the larger radius. This is typically used to help lift a weight. The mechanical advantage in this type of machine is the ratio of the large radius of the rod to the small radius of the rod. A colloquial term which is used to describe this type of machine is "winch".

Figure 4.11. Crank

Another type of compound machine is a linkage, which is a device that is able to convert one type of rotating motion (such as that of a crank) to another type of rotating motion (oscillatory, rotational, or reciprocating). This process, it should be noted, can be reversed. It is not permanent. So you can use a linkage to convert motion in order to turn a crank as well.

Figure 4.12. Linkages

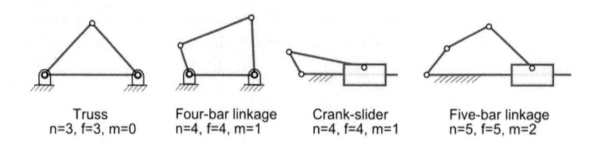

<table>
<tr><td align="center">Truss
n=3, f=3, m=0</td><td align="center">Four-bar linkage
n=4, f=4, m=1</td><td align="center">Crank-slider
n=4, f=4, m=1</td><td align="center">Five-bar linkage
n=5, f=5, m=2</td></tr>
</table>

5. Aviation and Nautical Information

While the Aviation & Nautical Information subtest consists of approximately 30 questions and lasts about 15 minutes (it is a computer adaptive test), the amount of knowledge required to obtain a good score is substantial. This subtest measures the applicant's knowledge of general aeronautical concepts and terminology which will require the majority of study time for this section. It also however includes questions regarding nautical information such as basic terminology and ability to identify parts of a ship or vessel. Most of the questions in this section will over aviation.

For the aviation portion, there are excellent online and printed study resources, including the Federal Aviation Administration's 281-page "Airplane Flying Handbook" (in pdf format at faa.gov). Instructional videos about aeronautics, aircraft structures and instruments, airports, and other AI topics are on YouTube.

For the Nautical portion, much like aviation, there is more information than could possibly be fit into a single book. There are many great free resources available online to supplement what you find in this book such as Wikipedia for the history of the US Navy which provides a great review of important facts and events. It is especially important to visit the Navy's website at www.navy.com and review in depth all the information there such as "Mission & History" and "Navy Equipment".

5.1– Types of aviation and aircraft categories

Since the early 20th century, two main types of aviation have developed: *civil* and *military*, both of which involve *fixed-wing* and *rotary-wing* aircraft. Fighter jets, bombers, airliners, and corporate jets are examples of the former, while the latter group includes helicopters, gyrocopters, and tilt-rotor flying machines.

An aircraft is a machine supported aloft by lift created by air flowing across *airfoil* surfaces, be they *wings* attached to an airplane's fuselage, a *propeller* rotated by gears connected to an engine drive shaft, or spinning helicopter *rotor blades*, or by *buoyancy*, as in the case of airships and hot air balloons.

In the United States, civilian aircraft are certified under the following categories: normal, utility, acrobatic, commuter, transport, manned free balloons, and special classes. Special Airworthiness Certificates are issued by the Federal Aviation Administration for the following categories: primary, restricted, multiple, limited, light-sport, experimental, special flight permit, and provisional.

Military aircraft are categorized by the mission they perform: air superiority, anti-submarine warfare, coastal and sea lane patrolling, electronic warfare, ground attack (close air support), interdiction, mid-air refueling, mine sweeping, reconnaissance, search and rescue, strategic bombing, surveillance, training, transport, and weather observation.

Aircraft structure and components

Fixed-wing aircraft – called airplanes, or informally, planes – have a fuselage, wings, and anempennage (tail). A nose section, including the cockpit and cabin comprise the *fuselage*. The*empennage* consists of a vertical stabilizer and an attached (hinged) *rudder* that can be movedleft or right by the pilot via cockpit controls (pedals), and a horizontal *stabilizer* and hinged*elevator* that is also under the pilot's control and moves up and down. Some aircraft, like the U.S. F-16 fighter jet, have an all-moving horizontal stabilizer-elevator called a *stabilator*.

The inboard portion of airplane wings have extendible sections called *flaps*, which are locatedalong the trailing (aft) edge. They are used to increase the wing's surface area and deflect theairflow downward, thereby augmenting lift at reduced speeds. With flaps extended, planes can take off and land at a lower velocity, which requires less runway.

Some airplanes have leading-edge *slats*, which are also extended to maintain lift at relatively low airspeeds. Like flaps, slats help an airplane takeoff and land at a lower velocity, allowing for operations on shorter runways. The C-17 strategic airlifter is an example of a militaryplane with slats and flaps.

On top of the wings of many turbine-powered aircraft are *spoilers*, hinged panels that move upward after landing and destroy the residual lift in order to put the plane's full weight on the landing gear and maximize tire friction on the runway, thereby enhancing deceleration.

High-performance airplanes often have one or more *air brakes* – also called *speed brakes* –to help decelerate the aircraft, and in flight, increase the rate of descent. For example, the F-15 fighter jet has a large airbrake on the top fuselage that extends after landing. Air brakes are not spoilers because they are not designed to destroy lift.

The main structural member inside each wing of an airplane is the *spar*, which runs the lengthof the wing. Larger wings usually have more than one spar to provide extra support. Shaped*ribs* are attached perpendicularly to the spar or spars in order to provide the wing with more structure and greater strength. A *skin* of aircraft aluminum (in most cases) is attached to theframework of spar(s) and ribs.

Airplanes that fly substantially below the speed of sound typically have wings that are *perpendicular* to the aircraft's longitudinal (nose-to-tail) axis. The wings of most jet planesare *swept* back to delay the drag associated with air compressibility at high subsonic speeds.Swept wings increase the performance of high-performance airplanes.

Some military aircraft have a *delta wing* (shaped like a triangle) while others have *variable- geometry wings*. In the case of the latter, the pilot swings the wings forward to a positionthat is roughly perpendicular to the fuselage for takeoff and landing and flight at low airspeeds, and back when flying at high subsonic, transonic, and supersonic velocities. TheAir Force's B-1B Lancer bomber is an example of variable-geometry airplane.

Toward the outer trailing edge of each wing is a hinged flight control surface called an *aileron* that moves up and down. Ailerons operate in a direction opposite to each other and control the plane's rolling motion around the longitudinal axis. Ailerons are used to perform banking turns.

A *trim tab* on the rear of the rudder, elevator, and one aileron (usually) act to change the aerodynamic load on the surface and reduce the need for constant pilot pressure on the control column (or joystick) and left and right pedal. Each trim tab is controlled by the pilot via a switch or wheel in the cockpit.

Regarding a source of thrust, most aircraft are powered by one or more *piston* or *turbine* engines. In terms of propulsion type, the latter group consists of *turboprop*, *turbojet*, and a *turbofan*. Fighter aircraft have one turbojet engine or a pair of them, each equipped with an *afterburner*, which provides an increase in thrust above non-afterburner full throttle (called military power).

The pilot controls engine operation (start, ground idle, checks, throttle movement, reverse thrust, shutdown) via switches and levers in the cockpit. The number of engine controls corresponds to the number of engines. In single- and multi-engine planes with adjustable pitch propellers, the blade angle is also controlled from the cockpit via levers.

Reverse thrust is a feature of turboprop and many jet-powered aircraft, including airliners, aerial tankers, and transport planes. Reverse thrust is used after landing to shorten the ground roll, the runway distance required by the decelerating airplane. Turboprop reverse thrust involves the rotation of propeller blades (three to six, typically) to a blade angle that causes air to be forced forward (away from the plane), not backward over the wings and tail surfaces, as happens when the aircraft taxis and during takeoff, climb, cruise, descent, and landing.

Reverse thrust on jet aircraft is achieved by temporarily directing the engine exhaust forward. After landing, the pilot moves the reverse thrust levers on the cockpit throttle quadrant, which causes two rounded metallic sections on the back end of each engine – called buckets, or clamshell doors – to pneumatically move and come together. When deployed, they stop the engine exhaust from going aft and direct the hot airflow forward at an angle.

Another type of reverse thrust on some jet aircraft involves pivoting doors located roughly half way along the engine. After landing, the pilot moves the reverse thrust levers, which causes the doors (four on each engine) to open. As with the buckets/clamshell doors, the result is exhaust deflected forward, which increases aircraft deceleration greatly.

Most aircraft land on wheels – called *landing gear* – and many types of planes have retractable wheels. Wheel retraction results in less drag when the aircraft is airborne. Fixed- and rotary-wing aircraft equipped with *skis* are able to land and maneuver on surfaces covered with snow and/or ice.

Airplanes that takeoff and land on water have *floats* attached to supports that are connected to the fuselage, or a *boat-like hull* on the bottom of the fuselage. *Amphibious* aircraft can take off and land on both land and water due to retractable wheels.

Rotary-wing aircraft have a *fuselage*, *tail*, and *fin* (in most cases), and *landing gear* (e.g., skids, wheels, inflatable floats). The most common type of rotary-wing aircraft is the helicopter.

5.2– Aerodynamics forces

There are four main aerodynamic forces that act on an aircraft when it is airborne: weight, lift, thrust, and drag.

The aircraft and everything in it – pilots, passengers, fuel, cargo, etc. – have mass (weight). Because of the earth's gravitational pull, the combined mass of the aircraft and its contents acts downward. From a physics perspective, the total weight force is deemed to act through the aircraft's *center of gravity*.

Aerodynamic loads associated with flight maneuvers and air turbulence affect the aircraft's weight. Whenever an aircraft flies a curved flight path at a certain altitude, the load factor (force of gravity, or "G") exerted on the airfoils (e.g., wings, rotor blades) is greater than the aircraft's total weight.

When a pilot turns an aircraft by banking (rolling) left or right, the amount of "G" increases. Banking further in order to turn more tightly causes the machine's effective weight ("G" loading) to increase more. An airplane banked 30 degrees weighs an additional 16 percent, but at 60 degrees of bank – a very steep turn – it weighs twice as much as it does in straight and level flight in smooth air.

Gusts produced by turbulent air can quickly impose aerodynamic forces that also increase the aircraft's "G" (weight) force.

Lift is the force that counteracts an aircraft's weight and causes the machine to rise into the air and stay aloft. Lift is produced by airfoils that move through the air at a speed sufficient to create a pressure differential between the two surfaces and a resulting upward force. Lift acts perpendicular to the direction of flight through the airfoil's *center of pressure*, or *center of lift*.

Thrust is an aircraft's forward force, which is created by one or more engines (the largest plane in the world, the Antonov An-225 Mriya, has six huge turbofan jet engines). In propeller-driven airplanes and rotary-wing aircraft, the power output of the engine(s) is transformed into rotary motion via one or more transmissions (gear boxes). Generally, thrust acts parallel to the aircraft's longitudinal axis.

Drag opposes thrust; it is a rearward-acting force caused by airflow passing over the aircraft's structure and becoming disrupted. Drag acts parallel to the *relative wind* and is a function of aircraft shape and size, its velocity and angle (inclination) in relation to airflow, and the air's mass, viscosity, and compressibility.

An aircraft's *total drag* is the sum of its *profile drag*, *induced drag*, and *parasite drag*. When total drag is the lowest, the aircraft experiences its maximum endurance (in straight and level flight), best rate of climb, and for helicopters, minimum rate-of-descent speed for autorotation.

Profile drag is the sum of *form drag* and *skin friction*. Form drag varies with air pressure around the aircraft and its cross-sectional shape. Skin friction is a function of the roughness of the outer surface of an aircraft (due to surface imperfections, protruding rivet heads, etc.).

Induced drag is a product of lift; stationary aircraft generate no such drag. However, as lift is created during acceleration along the runway or strip (in the case of airplanes) or increased rotor rpm and angle of attack (in the case of helicopters), the resulting pressure differential between the airfoil surfaces creates an air vortex at the wing's or rotor blade's tip. The vortex moves parallel to the aircraft's longitudinal axis and expands in diameter with distance from the airfoil. The effect of each vortex is a retarding aerodynamic force called induced drag.

Parts of an aircraft that do not contribute to the production of lift create *parasite drag* when the machine is moving. On airplanes, such components include the nose section and fuselage, landing gear, engine pylons and cowlings, vertical stabilizer, and rudder. On helicopters, the cockpit and cabin, landing skids or wheels, externally mounted engines (on some types), tailboom, and fin create parasite drag.

Scientific principles of relevance to aeronautics

Bernoulli's Principle

In 1738, a Swiss scientist named Daniel Bernoulli published a book entitled *Hydrodynamica* in which he explained that an increase in the inviscid flow of a fluid (i.e., the flow of an ideal, zero-viscosity liquid or gas) resulted in a decrease of static pressure exerted by the fluid. Bernoulli's famous equation is $P + \frac{1}{2}\rho v^2$ = a constant, where P = pressure (a force exerted divided by the area exerted upon); ρ (the Greek letter "rho") = the fluid's density; and v = the fluid's velocity.

The constant in Bernoulli's formula is derived from the scientific principle that energy cannot be created or destroyed – only its form can be changed – and a system's total energy does not increase or decrease.

Conservation laws – conservation of energy

Bernoulli's Principle is based on the conservation of energy, which says that in a steady flow the sum of all forms of mechanical energy – a fluid's potential energy plus its kinetic energy – along a streamline (e.g., a tube) is the same at all points. Thus, greater fluid flow rate (a higher speed) results in increased kinetic energy and dynamic pressure and reduced potential energy and static pressure.

An aircraft filled with fuel has a finite amount of energy. Through combustion in the engine, the fuel's heat energy is converted into kinetic energy, either in the form of jet exhaust or at least one rotating propeller (many types of planes have two or more propellers). Spinning helicopter rotor blades also have kinetic energy.

If an aircraft is airborne when it runs out of fuel, it still has potential energy as a function of its height above the ground. As the pilot noses down to keep air flowing over the airfoils (wings, rotor blades) and create lift, the aircraft's potential energy is transformed into kinetic energy.

Combining Bernoulli's Principle with the fact that airfoils provide lift at varying speeds during different phases of flight (takeoff, climb, cruise, descent, landing), the lift produced in a given instant can be calculated using the following equation: $L = \frac{1}{2}\rho v^2 A C_l$, where L = the lift force, $\frac{1}{2}\rho v^2$ was previously explained, A = the airfoil's area (length multiplied by width), and C_l is the coefficient of lift of the airfoil.

Pilots need to remember that the lifting force on their aircraft is proportional to the density(ρ) of air through which they fly (higher altitude = less dense air), the aircraft's speed, and airfoil angle of attack (AOA).

Conservation of mass

In the scientific field of fluid dynamics, it has been established that a fluid's mass cannot be created or destroyed within a flow of interest (e.g., airflow in sub-zero temperature conditions). Conservation of mass is mathematically expressed as the mass continuity equation.

Conservation of momentum

Momentum, an object's mass times its velocity, cannot be created or destroyed. However, it can be changed through an applied force. Because it involves magnitude and direction, momentum is a vector quantity. It is conserved in all three directions (longitudinally, laterally, and in terms of yaw) simultaneously.

Venturi Effect

To understand how a machine with airfoils can take to the air and remain airborne, we need to examine a phenomenon called the Venturi Effect. In the late 18th century, an Italian physicist, Giovanni Battista Venturi, conducted experiments with a pump and an unusual tube. The diameter of one end of the tube was constant and the circumference of the tube's central portion was smaller. Downstream from the bottleneck, the tube's diameter increased. It was as though someone had squeezed the center of the tube, creating a constriction.

Venturi noticed that as fluids moved through the tube, the flow rate increased or accelerated and the force, or static pressure, against the tube's surface decreased as the diameter became smaller. The opposite phenomenon — reduced flow rate (deceleration) and greater static pressure — happened as the tube diameter downstream of the constriction widened. Venturi published his findings in 1797 and the effect that he observed, measured, and wrote about became associated with his name.

It has certainly been integral to aviation since theadvent of gliding centuries ago.

If a Venturi tube is cut in half longitudinally, the curvature of the tube wall would look similarto that of an airplane wing's upper surface or the top of helicopter rotor blades. A moving airfoil "slices" the air, forcing molecules to travel to one side or the other. Those moving across the curved side have to travel a greater distance to reach the trailing edge than those moving across the relatively flat side. Consequently, the air molecules moving across the curved surface accelerate, as they did in Venturi's tube, and the static pressure drops.

Because pressure flows from high to low, the static pressure differential experienced between an airfoil's two sides imposes an aerodynamic force acting from the high-pressure(flat) surface to the low-pressure (curved) side. When acting upward, the force is called lift.

Newton's First Law of Motion
A stationary object remains at rest and an object in motion continues to move at the samerate (speed) and in the same direction unless acted upon by a force.

Newton's Second Law of Motion
Acceleration results from a force being applied to an object. The heavier the body, the greaterthe amount of force needed to accelerate it.

Newton's Third Law of Motion
Sir Isaac Newton (1642–1727) was a brilliant English physicist and mathematician who formulated universal laws of motion, including his third, which said that for every action thereis an equal and opposite reaction. Consequently, when an airfoil is deflected up, the airstreamflowing over the airfoil reacts by moving downward. Also, when exhaust from jet engines is directed backward the resulting reactive force on the engines, engine pylons, wings, and therest of the airplane is forward.

Aircraft motion occurs around three axes – longitudinal, lateral, and yaw – that go through the machine's center of gravity. The longitudinal axis has been explained; an aircraft rolls around it. The lateral axis is horizontal and perpendicular to the longitudinal axis; on basicairplane images it is depicted as a straight line going through one wingtip to the other. Theyaw axis is vertical; an aircraft is said to yaw (rotate) around it.

Flight control
When lift = weight and thrust = drag, the aircraft is either stationary on the ground, or aloft in straight-and-level, unaccelerated flight. To make an aircraft accelerate requires an increasein thrust, which the pilot controls from the cockpit by moving one or more throttle controls(on piston aircraft) or power lever(s) on turbine aircraft.

During takeoff, the airplane accelerates along the runway, strip, or body of water and reachesa speed at which it is going fast enough for the wings to generate lift. To make the plane go skyward, the pilot pulls back on the control column or joystick, which causes (via cables inlighter, smaller aircraft, or a hydraulic system in larger, heavier planes) the hinged elevatorto tilt up.

The inclined elevator forces air passing over it to deflect up, resulting in a downward reactionforce on the airplane's tail. Because the elevator is aft of the aircraft's center of gravity, as the tail drops the nose of the plane rises and the aircraft climbs.

To make the plane descend, the opposite happens.

To turn an airplane, the pilot moves the control wheel or joystick to the left or right (as desired) to change the machine's direction. The aileron on the wing on the plane's side towhere the pilot wants to turn rises into the airstream, forcing the flow upward and reducing the lift produced by the outer portion of the wing where the aileron is located. The result isa wing that drops, rolling (banking) the aircraft.

On the opposite side of the airplane, the aileron moves down into the airstream, deflectingthe airflow downward and creating more lift, which causes the wing to rise. With one wing down and the opposite wing up, the airplane rolls to the left or right.

For a coordinated banked turn, the pilot needs to move the aircraft's rudder to the side of the turn (left, right), which is accomplished by pushing on the corresponding pedal in frontof him or her. As the pilot does so, the airflow passing over the moved rudder is deflected tothe left or right, corresponding to the pushed pedal. The reactive force against the verticalstabilizer is opposite (right, left) and because the tail is aft of the plane's center of gravity,the nose yaws around the yaw axis in the opposite direction (left, right).

5.3– Additional aviation terms and definitions

Airfoil: A wing or helicopter blade that generates more lift than drag as air flows over its upperand lower surfaces. A propeller is also an airfoil. Airfoils are carefully designed and can be made of non-metallic materials such as composites.

Angle of attack: The angle between the chord line of an airfoil and its direction of motion relative to the air (i.e., the relative wind). AOA is an aerodynamic angle.

Angle of incidence: In the context of fixed-wing airplanes, the angle of incidence is the inclination of the wing or tail surface attached to the fuselage relative to an imaginary linethat is parallel to the aircraft's longitudinal axis.

Anhedral angle: The downward angle of an airplane's wings and tail plane from the horizontalis called the anhedral angle, or negative dihedral angle.

Attitude: An aircraft's position relative to its three axes and a reference such as the earth's horizon.

Center of gravity (CG): An aircraft's center of mass, the theoretical point through which theentire weight of the machine is assumed to be concentrated.

Chord: The distance between the leading and trailing edges along the chord line is an airfoil'schord. In the case of a tapered airfoil, as viewed from above, the chord at its tip will be different than at its root. Average chord describes the average distance.

Chord line: An imaginary straight line from the airfoil's leading (front) edge to its trailing (aft)edge.

Constant speed propeller: A controllable-pitch propeller whose angle is automatically changed in flight by a governor in order to maintain a constant number of revolutions perminute (rpm) despite changing aerodynamic loads.

Controllability: A measure of an aircraft's response relative to flight control inputs from thepilot.

Controllable pitch propeller: A propeller that can be varied in terms of its blade angle by thepilot via a control in the cockpit.

Coordinated flight: When the pilot applies flight and power control inputs to prevent slippingor skidding during any aircraft maneuver, the flight is said to be coordinated.

Critical angle of attack: The angle of attack at which an airfoil stalls (loses lift) regardless ofthe aircraft's airspeed, attitude, or weight.

Dihedral angle: The upward angle of an airplane's wings and tail plane from the horizontal.

Dihedral effect: The amount of roll moment produced per degree of sideslip is called dihedral effect, which is crucial in terms of an aircraft's rolling stability about its longitudinal axis.

Directional stability: An aircraft's initial tendency about its yaw (vertical) axis. When an aircraft is disturbed yaw-wise from its equilibrium state due to a gust, for example, and returns to that state (i.e., aligned with the relative wind) because of the aerodynamic effectof the vertical stabilizer, it is said to be directionally stable.

Downwash: Air that is deflected perpendicular to an airfoil's motion.

Drag coefficient: A dimensionless quantity that represents the drag generated by an airfoil ofa particular design.

Drag curve: A constructed image of the amount of aircraft drag at different airspeeds.

Dynamic stability: Describes the tendency of an aircraft after it has been disturbed fromstraight-and-level flight to restore the aircraft to its original condition of flying straight andlevel by developing corrective forces and moments.

Equilibrium: In the context of aviation, equilibrium is an aircraft's state when all opposing forces acting on it are balanced, resulting in unaccelerated flight at a constant altitude.

Feathering propeller: A controllable-pitch propeller that can be rotated sufficiently by thepilot (via a control lever in the cockpit connected to a governor in the propeller hub) so that the blade angle is parallel to the line of flight, thereby minimizing propeller drag.*Forward slip*: A pilot-controlled maneuver where the aircraft's longitudinal axis is inclined to its flight path.

Glide ratio: The ratio between altitude lost and distance traversed during non-powered flight(e.g., following an engine failure, in a sailplane).

Glidepath: An aircraft's path across the ground while approaching to land.

Gross weight: An aircraft's total weight when it is fully loaded with aircrew, fuel, oil, passengers and/or cargo (if applicable), weapons, etc.

Gyroscopic precession: The attribute of rotating bodies to manifest movement ninety degreesin the direction of rotation from the point where a force is applied to the spinning body.

Heading: The direction in which the aircraft's nose is pointed.

Inertia: A body's opposition to a change in motion.

Internal combustion engine: A mechanical device that produces power from expanding hotgases created by burning a fuel-air mixture within the device.

Lateral stability (rolling): An aircraft's initial tendency relative to its longitudinal axis afterbeing disturbed, its designed quality to return to level flight following a disturbance such asa gust that causes one of the aircraft's wings to drop.

Lift coefficient: A dimensionless quantity that represents the lift generated by an airfoil of aparticular design.

Lift/drag ratio: A number that represents an airfoil's efficiency, the ratio of the lift coefficientto the drag coefficient for a specific angle of attack.

Lift-off: The act of rising from the earth as a result of airfoils lifting the aircraft above the ground.

Load factor: The ratio of load supported by an aircraft's lift-generating airfoils (wings, mainrotor blades) to the aircraft's actual weight, including the mass of its contents. Load factor isalso known as G-loading ("G" means gravity).

Longitudinal stability: An aircraft's initial tendency relative to its lateral axis after beingdisturbed, its designed quality to return to its trimmed angle of attack after being disrupteddue to a wind gust or other factor.

Maneuverability: An aircraft's ability to change directions in three axes along its flight pathand withstand the associated aerodynamic forces.

Mean camber line: An imaginary line between the leading and trailing edges and halfway between the airfoil's upper (curved) and lower (flat) surfaces.

Minimum drag speed (L/DMAX): The point on the total drag curve where total drag is minimized and lift is maximized (i.e., where the lift-to-drag ratio is greatest).

Nacelle: An enclosure made of metal or another durable material that covers an aircraft engine.

Non-symmetrical airfoil (cambered): When one surface of an airfoil has a specific curvature that the opposite side does not, the airfoil is described as non-symmetrical, or cambered. Theadvantage of a non-symmetrical wing, for example, is that it produces lift at an AOA of zerodegrees (as long as airflow is moving past the blade). Moreover, the lift-to-drag ratio and stallcharacteristics of a cambered airfoil are better than those of a symmetrical airfoil. Its disadvantages are center of the pressure movement chord-wise by as much as one-fifth thechord line distance, which causes undesirable airfoil torsion, and greater production costs.

Normal category: An airplane intended for non-acrobatic operation that seats a maximum ofnine passengers and has a certificated takeoff weight of 12,500 pounds or less.

Payload: In the context of aviation, the weight of an aircraft's occupants, cargo, and baggage.

P-factor (precession factor): A propeller-driven aircraft's tendency to yaw to the left when the propeller rotates clockwise (as seen by the pilot) because the descending propeller bladeon the right produces more thrust than the ascending blade on the left. If the propeller rotated counter-clockwise, the yaw tendency would be to the right.

Piston engine: Also known as a reciprocating engine, it is a heat engine that uses one or more pistons to convert pressure created by expanding, hot gases resulting from a combusted fuel-air mixture, or steam pressure, into a rotating motion.

Pitch: An airplane's rotation about its lateral axis, or the angle of a propeller blade as measured from the vertical plane of rotation.

Power lever: The cockpit lever connected to a turbine engine's fuel control unit, which changes the amount of fuel entering the combustion chambers.

Powerplant: An engine and its accessories (e.g., starter-generator, tachometer drive) and theattached propeller (usually via a gearbox).

Propeller blade angle: The angle between the chord of an airplane propeller blade and thepropeller's plane of rotation.

Propeller lever: The cockpit control that controls propeller speed and angle.

Propeller slipstream: Air accelerated behind a spinning propeller.

Propeller: A relatively long and narrow blade-like device that produces thrust when it rotatesrapidly. In aviation, the term typically includes not only the propeller blades but also the huband other components that make up the propeller system.

Rate of turn: The rate of a turn expressed in degrees per second.

Reciprocating engine: An engine that converts heat energy created by combusted fuel mixedwith air into reciprocating piston movement, which in turn is converted into a rotary motionvia a crankshaft.

Reduction gear: A gear or set of gears that turns a propeller at a speed slower than that of the engine.

Relative wind: The direction of airflow relative to an airfoil, a stream of air parallel and opposite to an aircraft's flight path.

Ruddervator: Two control surfaces on an aircraft's tail that form a "V". When moved together via the control wheel or joystick in the cockpit, the surfaces act as elevators. When the pilotpresses his or her foot against one rudder pedal or the other, the ruddervator acts like aconventional plane's rudder.

Sideslip: A flight maneuver controlled by the pilot that involves the airplane's longitudinalaxis remaining parallel to the original flight path, but the aircraft no longer flies forward, asin normal flight. Instead, the horizontal lift component causes the plane to move laterally toward the low wing.

Skid: A flight condition during a turn where the airplane's tail follows a path outside of the path of the aircraft's nose.

Slip: A maneuver used by pilots to increase an aircraft's rate of descent or reduce its airspeed, and to compensate for a crosswind during landing. An unintentional slip also occurs when apilot does not fly the aircraft in a coordinated manner.

Stability: An aircraft's inherent tendency to return to its original flight path after a force suchas a wind gust disrupts its equilibrium. Aeronautical engineers design most aircraft to beaerodynamically stable.

Stall: A rapid decrease in lift caused by an excessive angle of attack and airflow separating from an airfoil's upper surface. An aircraft can stall at any pitch attitude or airspeed.

Standard-rate turn: A rate of turn of three degrees per second.

Subsonic: Speed below the speed of sound, which varies with altitude.

Supersonic: Speed in excess of the speed of sound, which varies with altitude.

Swept wing: A wing planform involving the tips being further back than the wing root.

Symmetrical airfoil: When an airfoil has identical upper and lower surfaces, it is symmetrical and produces no lift at an AOA of zero degrees. The wings of very high performance aircrafttend to be symmetrical.

Taxiway lights: Blue lights installed at taxiway edges.

Taxiway turn off lights: Green lights installed level with the taxiway.

Throttle: A mechanical device that meters the amount of fuel-air mixture fed to the engine.

Thrust line: An imaginary line through the center of an airplane's propeller hub and perpendicular to the propeller's plane of rotation, or through the center of each jet engine.

Total aerodynamic force (TAF): Two components comprise the total aerodynamic force: liftand drag. The amount of lift and drag produced by an airfoil are primarily determined by itsshape and area.

Torque: A propeller-driven airplane's tendency to roll in the opposite direction of the propeller's rotation. Some multi-engine airplanes have propellers that rotate in oppositedirections to eliminate the torque effect.

Trailing edge: The aft part of an airfoil where air that was separated as it hit the wing's frontedge and was forced over the upper and lower surfaces comes together.

Transonic: At the speed of sound, which varies with altitude.

Trim tab: A small, hinged control surface on a larger control surface (e.g., aileron, rudder, elevator) that can be adjusted in flight to a position that balances the aerodynamic forces. Instill air, a trimmed aircraft in flight requires no control inputs from the pilot to remain straightand level.

T-tail: The description for an airplane's tail involving the horizontal stabilizer mounted on thetop of the vertical stabilizer.

Turbulence: The unsteady flow of a fluid or gas (e.g., water or air).

Utility category: An airplane intended for limited acrobatic operation that seats a maximumof nine passengers and has a certificated takeoff weight of 12,500 pounds or less.

Vector: A force applied in a certain direction. Depicted visually, a vector shows the force's magnitude and direction.

Velocity: The rate of movement (e.g., miles per hour, knots) in a certain direction.

Vertical stability: An aircraft's designed, inherent behavior relative to its vertical axis, itstendency to return to its former heading after being disturbed by a wind gust or other disruptive force. Also called yawing or directional stability.

V-tail: A design involving two slanted tail surfaces that aerodynamically behave similar to a conventional elevator and rudder, i.e., as horizontal and vertical stabilizers.

Wing: An airfoil attached to a fuselage that creates a lifting force when the aircraft has reached a certain speed.

Wing area: A wing's total surface, including its control surfaces, and winglets, if so equipped.

Wing in ground effect (WIG): When an aircraft flies at a very low altitude, one roughly equalto its wingspan, it experiences WIG. The effect increases as the airplane descends closer tothe surface (runway, land, water) and supports the aircraft on a cushion of air best at analtitude of one half the wing span.

Winglet: A surface installed on a wingtip that is angled to the wing and improves its efficiencyby smoothing the airflow across the upper wing near the tip and reducing induced drag. Winglets improve an aircraft's lift-to-drag ratio.

Wing span: The maximum distance between wingtips.

Wingtip vortices: A spinning mass of air generated at a wing's tip created by outward-flowinghigh pressure air from underneath the wing meeting inward-flowing low air pressure on thewing's upper surface. The intensity of a wing vortex – also referred to as wake turbulence –is dependent on an airplane's weight, speed, and configuration.

Wing twist: A wing design feature that improves the effectiveness of aileron control at high angles of attack during an approach to a stall.

5.4– General Shipboard Directions & Parts of a Vessel

There are of course highly specialized parts of a Naval ship that are not found on a normal boat as shown below, but for purposes of the ASTB you should be familiar with the general concepts of the parts of a boat and directional information as found in the image below.

Figure 5.1. Parts of a boat

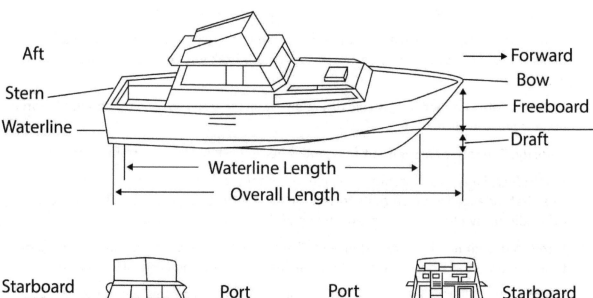

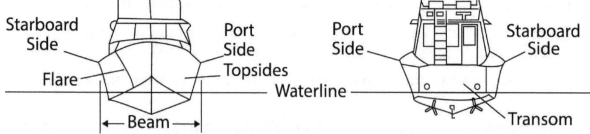

5.5 -Basic Nautical Terms

The following list of terms comprises some of the basic Naval terms you should be familiar with before taking the ASTB. There are of course many more specialized terms and acronyms used in the Marines, Navy, and Coast Guard, but for purposes of the ASTB, the below glossary, provided by the Navy (https://www.navy.com/glossary.html) is the extent of what you should be familiar with.

Table 5.1. Navy glossary

Adrift	Loose from moorings and out of control. Applied to anything lost or out of hand.
Aft	Towards the stern (tail) of a ship.
All hands	The entire ship's company, both officer and enlisted.
Allotment	An amount of money a sailor has coming out of regular pay.
Aye, aye	Response acknowledging the understanding of a command/statement.
Barracks	A building where sailors live when ashore.
Below	Downstairs, like the next deck below.
Black shoe	Non-aviation rate for enlisted personnel as well as officers. A "shoe" is a ship driver or surface warfare officer.
Blue nose	A sailor who has crossed either the Arctic or Antarctic Circle. Also applies to officers.
Bow	The forward part of a ship or boat.
Bravo zulu	Naval term for "well done".
Bright work	Brass or shiny metal kept polished rather than painted.
Brown shoe	Aviation rate enlisted personnel.
Bulkhead	The wall.
Bunk	A bed.
Buoy	An anchored float used as an aid to navigation or to mark the location of an object.
Carry on	An order to resume work or duties.
Cast off	To throw off, to let go, to unfurl.
Chain locker	Compartment in which anchor chain is stowed.

Chit	Forms used to request taking leave, a day off, etc.
Chit book	Coupon or receipt booklet.
Colors	Raising and lowering of the National Ensign, the American flag and organization flags.
Cup of Joe	A cup of coffee. Named after Josephus Daniels, Secretary of the Navy 1913–1921, who under General Order 99 in June 1914 prohibited the use of alcohol on board U.S. Navy ships.
Deck	The floor.
Deep six	To dispose of or throw away.
Enlisted	The general workforce of the Navy and Navy Reserve – generally requires a high school diploma (or GED) as a minimum educational requirement, completion of Recruit Training and training in an occupational specialty area.
Ensign	The rank of an Officer between Chief Warrant Officer and Lieutenant Junior Grade.
Fast	Snugly secured.
Fathom	A unit of length equal to six feet, used for measuring the depth of water.
Field day	Full-blown cleaning, sort of like spring cleaning in overdrive.
First lieutenant	The officer responsible to the XO for the deck department/division aboard ship.
Flag officer	Any commissioned officer in pay grade 0–7 or above.
Galley	The kitchen.
Gangway	An opening in the bulwark or lifeline that provides access to a brow or accommodation ladder; when shouted means to get out of the way.
Gear locker	A storage room.
General quarters	Battle stations.
Ground tackle	The equipment used for mooring or anchoring a ship.
Hatch	The door.
Head	The restroom.

Jack box	Access box to sound-powered phone circuitry.
Leave	Authorized absence.
Liberty	Permission to leave base, usually for not more than forty-eight hours.
Lifeline	Lines erected around the weather decks of a ship to prevent personnel from falling or being washed over the side.
Marlin spike	A life-size model ship where recruits practice mooring, line handling, putting out to sea and other aspects of basic seamanship.
Mess deck	Cafeteria.
Mess duty	A ninety-day obligated duty working on the mess decks when first reporting aboard. (aka mess crank'n).
Mid-watch	The midnight watch, the most dreaded watch because one loses the most sleep out of the rotation.
Navy reserve	Reserve component of the U.S. Navy in which part-time Sailors and Officers are called into Active Duty, or mobilized, as needed.
Ombudsman	Volunteer who is the well-trained link between sailors and their families.
Port	A place on a waterway with facilities for loading and unloading ships.
Port side	The left side of a nautical vessel.
Quarters	Assembling all hands for muster. Also refers to a home on base, a residence.
Rack	A bed.
Rating	A job specialty title.
Reveille	A signal signifying the start of a workday.
Scullery	A place to wash dishes.
Scuttlebutt	Originally meant to describe a water fountain. Quickly became a place Sailors would gather and talk. Term now used primarily for rumors and rumor control.
Secure	To stop or quit work.
Sick bay	Medical facility on a nautical vessel.

Snipe	Name for anyone who works in the engineering department.
Starboard	The right side of a nautical vessel.
Stern	The aft (rear) part of a ship or boat.
Swab	A mop.
Taps	Lights out.
Turn to	Begin work.
Working aloft	Working above the highest deck, generally performing maintenance on the ship's mast.

6. Practice Test One

Paragraph Comprehension

Young Conrad's birthday was fixed for his espousals. The company was assembled in the chapel of the Castle, and everything ready for beginning the divine office, when Conrad himself was missing. Manfred, impatient of the least delay, and who had not observed his son retire, dispatched one of his attendants to summon the young Prince. The servant, who had not stayed long enough to have crossed the court to Conrad's apartment, came running back breathless, in a frantic manner, his eyes staring, and foaming at the month. He said nothing, but pointed to the court.

The Castle of Otranto by Horace Walpole

1. What is the general mood of this passage?

   a. Happy

   b. Depressing

   c. Frantic

   d. hopeful

2. On which day was Conrad to be married?

   a. The birthday of his wife

   b. His own birthday

   c. His father's birthday

   d. The day after his birthday

In the past, many cars were powered by manual transmissions. Today, however, most cars have shifted to an automatic transmission. Shifting gears in a manual, however, is an important skill to learn if you plan to hit the road. Simply depress the clutch and then shift with the shifting lever to get the right gear. Then release the clutch and apply pressure to the gas at the same time.

3. Why have cars shifted from manual to automatic transmissions?

   a. Manual transmissions no longer work.

   b. Manual transmissions are too complex.

   c. Automatic transmissions are cheaper.

   d. There is not enough information to determine why.

4. What is the second step when shifting gears in a manual transmission?

   a. Manual transmissions no longer work.

   b. Manual transmissions are too complex.

   c. Automatic transmissions are cheaper.

   d. There is not enough information to determine why.

5. What is the second step when shifting gears in a manual transmission?

   a. Press the gas.

   b. Press the clutch.

   c. Move the shifting lever.

   d. Press the brake.

6. What kind of transmission do most modern cars have?

   a. Automatic

   b. Manual

   c. Shifting

   d. Auto gear

These visions faded when I perused, for the first time, those poets whose effusions entranced my soul and lifted it to heaven. I also became a poet and for one year lived in a paradise of my own creation; I imagined that I also might obtain a niche in the temple where the names of Homer and Shakespeare are consecrated. You are well acquainted with my failure and how heavily I bore the disappointment. But just at that time I inherited the fortune of my cousin, and my thoughts were turned into the channel of their earlier bent.

Frankenstein by Mary Shelley

7. Why did the narrator stop having visions?

    a. He discovered poetry.

    b. He died.

    c. He went to heaven.

    d. His soul was lost.

8. Where did the narrator live after becoming a poet?

    a. His house

    b. A paradise of his own creation

    c. A temple

    d. None of the above

Jim was going to the store to buy apples when he was sidetracked. Sally had been following him the entire time and finally decided to call out. Jim has broken up with her for a reason, and it was ridiculous to think she was still trying to get his attention.

9. Why might Jim not be happy to see Sally?

    a. He is too busy to talk to her.

    b. She hates apples.

    c. They broke up.

    d. She hates him.

The House of Representatives shall be composed of Members chosen every second Year by the People of the several States, and the Electors in each State shall have the Qualifications requisite for Electors of the most numerous Branch of the State Legislature.

The United States Constitution

10. How often are the members of the House of Representatives elected?

    a. Every four years

    b. Every three years

    c. Every year

    d. Every two years

When in the Course of human events, it becomes necessary for one people to dissolve the political bands which have connected them with another, and to assume among the powers of the earth, the separate and equal station to which the Laws of Nature and of Nature's God entitle them, a decent respect to the opinions of mankind requires that they should declare the causes which impel them to the separation.

The Declaration of Independence

11. What is this paragraph introducing?

    a. Reasons for a separation

    b. Reasons to stay together

    c. A revolution

    d. Human history

12. Which of the following might mean the same as dissolve political bands?

    a. Make a treaty

    b. Eliminate the government

    c. Abolish slavery

    d. Move away

Vampires are known to be wary of men who have, on their person, garlic, crosses, holywater, or bibles. They tend to steer clear of these men, as they see them as dangerous to their continued existence.

13. Which of the following do vampires avoid?

    a. Garlic

    b. Holy water

    c. Crosses

    d. All of the above

No Senator or Representative shall, during the Time for which he was elected, be appointed to any civil Office under the Authority of the United States, which shall have been created, or the Emoluments whereof shall have been increased during such time; and no Person holding any Office under the United States, shall be a Member of either House during his Continuance in Office.

The United States Constitution

14. What does this mean in simple terms?

    a. Representatives cannot create jobs for themselves.

    b. Representatives cannot be paid.

    c. Representatives cannot be civil servants.

    d. Representatives must quit their jobs.

Today was not a good day. It all started with the rain in the morning. The windows were down on the car, so the seats got all wet. Then the call from Juliet, and the breakup. After that, I lost my job. Today was not a good day at all.

15. What was the last sign that *today was not a good day*?

    a. Rain

    b. Wet car seat

    c. Call from Juliet

    d. Lost job

When Dr. Van Helsing and Dr. Seward had come back from seeing poor Renfield, we went gravely into what was to be done. First, Dr. Seward told us that when he and Dr. Van Helsing had gone down to the room below they had found Renfield lying on the floor, all in a heap. His face was all bruised and crushed in, and the bones of the neck were broken.

Dracula by Bram Stoker

16. What does the narrator mean by *went gravely into what was to be done*?

    a. They have to kill each other.

    b. They have to go to a grave.

    c. They have to dig a grave.

    d. They have to make a plan.

Every year the Academy Awards, or better known as the Oscars, brings together the best of the best in Hollywood. Each year since the original awards ceremony in 1929 great achievements in all areas of the film industry are recognized. Many married female actors, however, shy away from the honor of winning the Academy Award of Merit for either Best Actress or Best Supporting Actress. Ever since 1935, the "Oscar Curse" has proven more often than not to be alive and well.

17. What is the "Oscar Curse" that these famous ladies of Hollywood fear?

    a. After winning they will meet an untimely end.

    b. After winning their husbands' will leave them.

    c. Their next movie will be a box-office disaster.

    d. Once they win, they will never again win in the same category.

According to CNN.com, Google recently announced that it is developing smart contact lenses that will measure a diabetic's glucose level by testing the person's tears. If victorious, Google will eliminate a very laborious daily routine in every diabetic's life; drawing blood from their body (usually from the side of a finger) to test their glucose levels.

18. In this paragraph what does the word *laborious* mean?

    a. Consuming too much time

    b. Needing unwelcome, often tedious effort

    c. Needing to be done in a medical laboratory

    d. An excruciatingly painful procedure

Ikea stores have a unique section in their parking lots. They have a "family friendly" parking area. This area is located very close to the front entrance to the store. These spots have pink strollers painted on each parking spot.

19. What is implied by the term *family friendly*?

    a. Only customers with young children can park in this area.

    b. If you have an Ikea family membership you are welcome to park in this area.

    c. Any family of any age is welcome to park in this area.

    d. If there are only a few parking spots left in this area, it would be polite to leave it available for a family, but it's not the rule.

Everyone dreams of winning the lottery; one million, 25 million, even 55 million dollars. It is very easy to get caught up in the dreams associated with winning the jackpot. The realists of the world, however, are quick to remind us that we have a better chance of being hit by a car than winning big with the lottery.

20. What does the comparison of winning the lottery to being hit by a car imply?

    a. If you don't have the good luck to win the lottery, watch out because you are likely to get hit by a car.

    b. It is not lucky to either win the lottery or be hit by a car.

    c. More people will get hit by a car than will win the lottery.

    d. If you buy a lottery ticket, don't walk anywhere.

The United States Military Academy at West Point (USMA) is better known as the Point. Dating back to 1802, this coeducational federal service academy has trained some of the most revered and honored military leaders in American history. West Point has a Cadet Honor Code that is almost as old as the academy itself; "A Cadet will not lie, cheat, steal, or tolerate those who do."

21. What is the foundation of the Honor Code of West Point?

    a. The foundation of the Honor Code comes from a time when the United States where divided by the conflicts leading up to the American Civil War, but were training soldiers from both sides of the Mason-Dixie Line. This Code was required to prevent men from fighting amongst themselves.

    b. This code came from the Southern Gentleman's Guide to Behavior and introduced to men from the northern states during the early years of the academy.

    c. The Honor Code of West Point was adopted from the British Military's Training Manual that was created years before West Point even existed.

    d. West Point's Code of Honor dates back to the beginning of the academy when a gentlemen's word was considered his bond. To break one's word was the worst possible thing a gentleman could ever do. His word was his honor, and without honor a man was nothing.

Mathematics Knowledge

1. Simplify the expression $(5x^2)^{10}$.

   a. $5^{10}x^{20}$

   b. $(5x)^{12}$

   c. $5x^{-8}$

   d. $50x^2$

2. Evaluate the expression $\frac{x^2-2y}{y}$ when $x = 20$ and $y = 10$.

   a. 0

   b. 38

   c. 36

   d. 19

3. Adam is painting the outside of a 4-walled shed. The shed is 5 feet wide, 4 feet deep, and 7 feet high. How much paint will Adam need if he includes the top of the shed?

   a. 126 ft^2

   b. 140 ft^3

   c. 63 ft^2

   d. 46 ft

4. Liz is installing a tile backsplash. If each tile is a right isosceles triangle with two sides that measure 6 centimeters in length, how many tiles does she need to cover an area of 1800 square centimeters?

   a. 36 tiles

   b. 100 tiles

   c. 50 tiles

   d. 300 tiles

5. $2.31 \times 10^2 =$

    a. 23.1

    b. 231

    c. 2310

    d. 23100

6. If $f(x) = |x - 28|$, evaluate $f(-12)$.

    a. −16

    b. 40

    c. 16

    d. −40

7. $10^8 \div 10^3 =$

    a. 10^5

    b. 10^6

    c. 10^{11}

    d. 10^{10}

8. What is 15% of 986?

    a. 146.9

    b. 98.6

    c. 9.86

    d. 147.9

9. A circular swimming pool has a circumference of 49 feet. What is the diameter of the pool?

    a. 15.6 feet

    b. 12.3 feet

    c. 7.8 feet

    d. 17.8 feet

10. 50% of 94 is:

    a. 42

    b. 52

    c. 45

    d. 47

11. If ∡A measures 57 degrees, find ∡G.

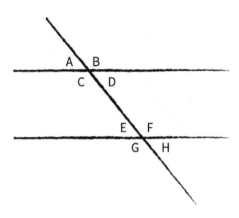

    a. 57 degrees

    b. 147 degrees

    c. 123 degrees

    d. 33 degrees

12. The table below shows the number of hours worked by employees during the week. What is the median number of hours worked per week by the employees?

Employee	Suzanne	Joe	Mark	Ellen	Jill	Rob	Nicole	Dina
Hours worked per week	42	38	25	50	45	46	17	41

    a. 38

    b. 41

    c. 42

    d. 41.5

13. Multiply the following terms: $(11xy)(2x^2y)$

      a. $13xy + x$

      b. $22x^3y^2$

      c. $44x^3y^3$

      d. $22xy^2 + 2x^2$

14. $y = 2x - 5$, $x = 10$. What is y?

      a. 10

      b. 20

      c. 15

      d. 5

15. $x = 2$, $y = -3$, $z = 4$. Solve $x + y \times z$.

      a. -4

      b. 10

      c. -12

      d. -10

16. Factor the expression: $64 - 100x^2$.

      a. $(8 + 10x)(8 - 10x)$

      b. $(8 + 10x)^2$

      c. $(8 - 10x)^2$

      d. $(8 + 10x)(8x + 10)$

17. Which expression would you solve first in the following expression? $(9 + 9) \times 987 + 4^6$

      a. 4^6

      b. $(9 + 9)$

      c. 9×987

      d. $987 + 4$

18. Solve for y: $10y - 8 - 2y = 4y - 22 + 5y$

    a. $y = -4\frac{2}{3}$

    b. $y = 14$

    c. $y = 30$

    d. $y = -30$

19. Solve for x: $(2x + 6)(3x - 15) = 0$.

    a. $x = -5, 3$

    b. $x = -3, 5$

    c. $x = -2, -3$

    d. $x = -6, 15$

20. Round 0.1938562 to the nearest tenth.

    a. 0.0

    b. 0.2

    c. 0.19

    d. 0.194

21. Points B and C are on a circle, and a chord is formed by line segment $\overline{BC}$. If the distance from the center of the circle to point B is 10 centimeters, and the distance from the center of the circle to the center of line segment $\overline{BC}$ is 8 centimeters, what is the length of line segment $\overline{BC}$?

    a. 6 cm

    b. 4 cm

    c. 12 cm

    d. 14 cm

22. If $f(x) = 3^x - 2$, evaluate $f(5)$.

    a. 27

    b. 243

    c. 241

    d. 13

23. If a spherical water balloon is filled with 113 milliliters of water, what is the approximate radius of the balloon? (Note: The volume, V, of a sphere with radius r is found using the equation $V = \frac{4}{3}\pi r^3$.)

    a. 4.0 cm

    b. 3.0 cm

    c. 3.6 cm

    d. 3.3 cm

24. Simplify $\frac{13}{26}$ into a decimal.

    a. 0.13

    b. 0.16

    c. 0.5

    d. 0.25

25. Factor the expression $100x^2 + 25x$ using a greatest common factor.

    a. $100x(x + 25x)$

    b. $25(4x + x)$

    c. $25x(4x + 1)$

    d. $25(4x^2 + x)$

26. $F(x) = 6x - 3$, $G(x) = 3x + 4$

What will be $F(3) - G(2)$?

    a. 4

    b. 3

    c. 5

    d. 2

27. The mean of the marks obtained by the students in a class is 60 out of 100, and the standard deviation is 0. It means that

    a. Half of the students have scored marks less than 60.

    b. Half of the students have scored marks greater than 60.

    c. No student has scored 100 marks.

    d. All the students have scored 60 marks each.

28. 0.00092×10^{-3} is equal to which of the following?

    a. 0.000093×10^{-4}

    b. 0.000092×10^{-2}

    c. 0.000000092

    d. 0.92×10^{-8}

29. The remainder is 3 when we divide one number by another number. What can be these two numbers from the following?

    a. 9, 5

    b. 8, 5

    c. 9, 6

    d. Both B and C

30. If A and B are odd integers. Which of the following expressions must give an odd integer?

    a. $A \times B$

    b. $A + B$

    c. $A - B$

    d. Both A and C

85

Mechanical Comprehension

1. What is the formula that is used to calculate work?

   a. $W = F \times s$

   b. $W = v \times F$

   c. $W = P \times s$

   d. $W = P \times F$

2. If an engine with a power output of around 2 horsepower is 95% efficient, what would the actual power output be, in horsepower?

   a. 190

   b. 95

   c. 1.90

   d. 0.19

3. A class 2 lever has the load placed between the fulcrum/pivot point and the effort being placed on it. Which of these might be an example of this?

   a. wheelbarrow

   b. gun

   c. wrench

   d. screwdriver

4. One of the following materials is a ceramic, which one is it?

   a. dirt

   b. gold

   c. pots

   d. brick

5. Force per unit of distance is a description of what?

    a. velocity

    b. force fields

    c. power

    d. work

6. Which one of the following might be a good example of a simple machine?

    a. ladder

    b. drill

    c. jackhammer

    d. iPod

7. A machine is operating with an input (for work) of 215-foot pounds. The output of the work for this machine is 204.25-foot pounds. What efficiency does this machine have, considering the information above?

    a. 90%

    b. 95%

    c. 100%

    d. 200%

8. If there are 20 lbs. on one side of a fulcrum (with equal lengths on both sides), which of the following combinations of weights would be enough to balance the loads on that fulcrum?

    a. 18 and 1

    b. 18 and 2

    c. 18 and 3

    d. 12 and 18

9. What kind of machine would a cam be considered?

    a. difficult

    b. simple

    c. conductor

    d. compound

10. How would you find an exerted force?

    a. find the force using the formula for work

    b. use the force field formula

    c. multiply applied force by the ratio of the areas to which it is being applied

    d. none of the above

11. What is a linkage?

    a. a way of converting rotating motion of a crank

    b. a type of fence

    c. a way to move chains

    d. a pulley system of complex design

12. Which of the following is a description of mechanical advantage?

    a. input force * output force

    b. output force * input force

    c. output force / input force

    d. input force / output force

13. If someone puts in 50 newtons of force and gets back 250 newtons of force, then what is the mechanical advantage?

    a. 5

    b. 10

    c. 15

    d. 20

14. What is the name of the force between objects that attracts them together?

    a. friction

    b. gravity

    c. force

    d. power

15. What might cause an object to accelerate?

   a. force

   b. gravity

   c. pulling on it

   d. all of the above

16. What amount of force would have to be applied to move a box 25 meters? 55,000 joules worth of work is utilized in the process of moving the box.

   a. 2500 newtons

   b. 4000 newtons

   c. 2200 newtons

   d. 5500 newtons

17. What is heat?

   a. a type of motion

   b. a type of pressure

   c. a type of energy

   d. the result of friction

18. If two liquids that have different densities are mixed together, what will happen?

   a. they will separate

   b. they will combine into one fluid

   c. they will react violently

   d. they will flow out of the container

19. What is the SI unit that is commonly used to measure mass?

   a. liter

   b. kilograms

   c. newtons

   d. all of the above

20. When would a spring likely be utilized?

    a.   when making a large volleyball

    b.   when creating a football

    c.   when making a new baseball bat

    d.   when building a pogo stick

21. When people are using a seesaw, the seesaw will work most efficiently if the two people have the same weight. Why?

    a.   principle of equilibrium

    b.   principle of force

    c.   Newton's law

    d.   the first law of motion

22. Shock absorption on vehicles is attributed to what?

    a.   elasticity of springs

    b.   brakes

    c.   the engine block

    d.   the weight of the vehicle

23. What type of device would you compare a crane to?

    a.   car

    b.   elevator

    c.   pulley

    d.   lever

24. If you were going to make something that was solid but would not float, what might you use?

    a.   plastic

    b.   glass

    c.   metal

    d.   wood

25. How do brakes slow vehicles down?

    a. force

    b. combustion

    c. acceleration

    d. friction

26. Which of the following is not a correct unit for the amount of work done:

    a. Joule

    b. Horsepower-hour

    c. Calorie

    d. Newton

27. Observe the figure:

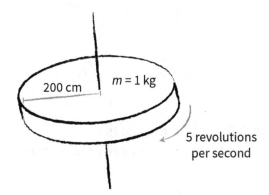

The kinetic energy of the disc is:

    a. $80\,\pi^2$ J

    b. $100\,\pi^2$ J

    c. $125\,\pi^2$ J

    d. $144\,\pi^2$ J

28. Consider the following figure of a rolling wheel on smooth horizontal surface:

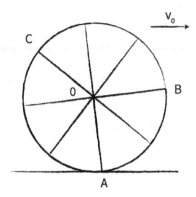

Then,

i.   Speed at the point A is 0

ii.   Speed at point B and C = vo

iii. Speed at point B > Speed at point O

    a. All the statements are true

    b. Only statement (i) & (ii) are true

    c. Only statement (i) & (iii) are true

    d. Only statement (ii) & (iii) are true

29. In the following figure, consider a block of mass *m*. What is the ratio of the force required for a person to lift the block upwards with and without a pulley? (Hint: Assume F = T)

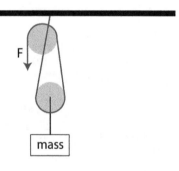

    a. 2

    b. 1/3

    c. 3

    d. 1/2

30. A block of mass 3kg lies on a horizontal surface with $\mu = 0.7$. Select the force closest to what is required just to move the block:

    a.   15N

    b.   21N

    c.   18N

    d.   24N

Aviation and Nautical Information

1. A propeller-driven airplane:

   a. Is part of the rotary class of aircraft (because the propeller spins).

   b. Has a reciprocating engine only.

   c. Is a fixed-wing aircraft.

   d. Has a reverse thrust feature in all types of military and civilian aircraft.

2. Military aircraft are categorized:

   a. As normal, utility, acrobatic, special mission, or transport.

   b. Based on the mission they perform.

   c. In accordance with Department of Defense directives since 1947.

   d. None of the above.

3. A propeller is:

   a. An airfoil.

   b. A secondary source of thrust.

   c. Part of a balanced thrust system involving only 2, 4, or 6 blades.

   d. An extendible thrust-generation device used at high altitudes.

4. The four main forces acting on an aircraft are:

   a. Deflection, exponential thrust, torque, and the total mass vector modified by the earth's Coriolis Effect.

   b. Lift, weight, thrust, and drag.

   c. Wind gusts, gravity, pressure differentials, and tangential rotation.

   d. All of the above.

5. Turbine aircraft:

   a. Have a propeller source of thrust in some cases.

   b. Never have a propeller source of thrust (only jets are turbine aircraft).

   c. Have a turbocharged engine.

   d. Utilize a ducted wind fan that spins an electrical generator.

6. The empennage consists of:

   a. A vertical stabilizer and a hinged rudder.

   b. The back half of the fuselage and the tail plane.

   c. The "T" tail and nacelle.

   d. The ruddervator and associated hydraulic system.

7. Flaps are used:

   a. To decrease Dutch roll.

   b. To eliminate wingtip vortices.

   c. During takeoff only.

   d. None of the above.

8. Hinged wing panels that move upward and destroy lift after landing are called:

   a. Air brakes.

   b. Spoilers.

   c. Winglets.

   d. Vertical stabilizers.

9. Swept-back wings:

   a. Delay the drag associated with air compressibility at approach speeds.

   b. Delay the drag associated with air compressibility at low subsonic speeds.

   c. Delay the drag associated with air compressibility at high subsonic speeds.

   d. All of the above.

10. Profile drag is the sum of:

   a. Skin friction and form drag.

   b. Skin friction and induced drag.

   c. Form drag and supplementary drag.

   d. Parasite drag and vortex drag.

11. Slats are located:

    a. Along the horizontal stabilizer's leading edge.

    b. Along the leading edge of both wings and the horizontal stabilizer.

    c. Along the trailing edge of the right aileron.

    d. Along the leading edge of both wings.

12. The laws of conservation that pertain to aircraft are:

    a. The law of conservation of mass, kinetic energy, and fluid flow.

    b. The law of conservation of mass, torque, and potential energy.

    c. The law of conservation of weight, thrust, and lift.

    d. The law of conservation of mass, energy, and momentum.

13. According to 18th century Swiss scientist Daniel Bernoulli:

    a. Accelerated fluid flow results in a decrease of dynamic pressure.

    b. Accelerated fluid flow results in a decrease of static pressure.

    c. Accelerated fluid flow results in an increase of total system energy.

    d. All of the above.

14. Lift produced by an airfoil is proportional to:

    a. The rate of air compressibility and the coefficients of lift and drag.

    b. The angle of airflow deflection, the relative wind's vertical vector component, and thereduction of induced drag as the aircraft accelerates.

    c. Air density, aircraft speed, wing area, and airfoil shape.

    d. None of the above.

15. The angle of attack is:

    a. The chord line's orientation in relation to the aircraft's longitudinal axis.

    b. The acute angle between the chord line of an airfoil and the relative wind.

    c. The sum of the angle of incidence of the wings and tail plane.

    d. The aircraft's downward inclination when shooting targets on the ground.

16. Parasite drag is produced by:

  a. Extended slats and flaps.

  b. Aircraft parts that do not contribute to producing lift.

  c. Improperly set trim tabs.

  d. A difference in propeller rpm on multi-engine airplanes.

17. Thrust opposes:

  a. Drag.

  b. Rudder deflection.

  c. Gyroscopic precession.

  d. Gravity.

18. Ailerons move:

  a. In opposing directions.

  b. Downward.

  c. Up or down, depending on the rudder pedal pushed by the pilot.

  d. None of the above.

19. The main types of turbine propulsion are:

  a. Axial and centrifugal flow.

  b. Non-afterburning, after burning, and turbocharged.

  c. Turbofan, turbojet, and turboprop.

  d. Turbocharged, turbofan, and ramjet.

20. An aircraft's three axes are:

  a. Longitudinal, gyroscopic, and lateral.

  b. Directional, pitch, and gyroscopic.

  c. Yaw, longitudinal, and lateral.

  d. Deflectional, lateral, and induced.

21. Increasing an aircraft's bank in a coordinated turn, _____ its _____ and

_____:

    a. increases; angle of attack; lift.

    b. increases; weight (due to "G" loading); rate of turn.

    c. decreases; angle of attack; drag.

    d. decreases; weight (due to "G" loading); angle of attack.

22. When the pilot pulls back on the control column or joystick:

    a. The elevator moves up.

    b. The elevator moves down.

    c. The left aileron moves down.

    d. None of the above.

23. To move the rudder to the right, the pilot:

    a. Turns the control wheel to the right.

    b. Pulls back on the right power lever.

    c. Moves the right throttle lever forward while pushing the right pedal.

    d. Pushes the right pedal.

24. From a physics perspective, an aircraft's total weight force is deemed to act through the

_____:

    a. Weight and balance reference datum.

    b. Center of pressure.

    c. Center of gravity.

    d. Center of momentum.

25. An air vortex at the wing tip creates:

    a. Form drag.

    b. Profile drag.

    c. Induced drag.

    d. Parasite drag.

26. Momentum is:

    a. An object's mass times its velocity squared.

    b. An object's mass times its velocity.

    c. An object's weight plus one-half of its velocity squared.

    d. An object's forward velocity times its coefficient of lift.

27. When exhaust from jet engines is directed backward, the resulting reactive force on the airplane is _____:

    a. Forward.

    b. Forward but deflected downward due to the angle of incidence.

    c. Forward but reduced because of the inclined component of the total drag vector.

    d. Determined only by using the conservation of energy equation.

28. Coordinated flight is defined as:

    a. The pilot applying control inputs that are suitable for the aircraft's density altitude.

    b. The pilot applying flight and power control inputs to prevent slipping or skiddingduring any aircraft maneuver.

    c. The pilot reducing back pressure on the control column or joystick while turning in theopposite direction of the horizontal component of total drag.

    d. All of the above.

29. Anhedral angle is the _____ angle of an airplane's wings and tail plane from the horizontal:

    a. Upward.

    b. Obtuse.

    c. Downward.

    d. Isosceles.

30. Minimum drag speed corresponds to:

    a. The point on the total drag curve where the thrust-to-drag ratio is least.

    b. The point on the total drag curve where the drag-to-mass ratio is least.

    c. The point on the total drag curve where the lift-to-drag ratio is greatest.

    d. The point on the total drag curve where the lift-to-weight ratio is least.

Practice Test One Answer Key

Paragraph Comprehension

1. C.

2. B.

3. D.

4. C.

5. A.

6. A.

7. B.

8. C.

9. D.

10. A.

11. B.

12. D.

13. A.

14. D.

15. D.

16. C.

17. B.

18. A.

19. D.

20. D.

Mathematics Knowledge

1. A.
2. B.
3. A.
4. B.
5. B.
6. B.
7. A.
8. D.
9. A.
10. D.
11. C.
12. D.
13. B.
14. C.
15. D.
16. A.
17. B
18. B.
19. B.
20. B.
21. C.
22. C.
23. B.
24. C.
25. C.
26. C.
27. D.
28. B.
29. D.
30. A.

Mechanical Comprehension

1. A.
2. C.
3. A.
4. D.
5. D.
6. A.
7. B.
8. B.
9. D.
10. C.
11. A.
12. C.
13. A.
14. B.
15. D.
16. C.
17. C.
18. A.
19. B.
20. D.
21. A.
22. A.
23. B.
24. C.
25. D.
26. D.
27. B.
28. C.
29. D.
30. B.

Aviation and Nautical Information

1. C.
2. B.
3. A.
4. B.
5. A.
6. A.
7. D.
8. B.
9. C.
10. A.
11. D.
12. D.
13. B.
14. C.
15. B.
16. B.
17. A.
18. A.
19. C.
20. C.
21. B.
22. A.
23. D.
24. C.
25. C.
26. B.
27. A.
28. B.
29. C.
30. C.

7. Practice Test Two

Paragraph Comprehension

Davy Crockett is one of America's best-known folk heroes. Known for his political contributions to the State of Tennessee and the U.S. Congress, he also became famous during his own time for "larger than life" exploits that were retold through plays and in almanacs. Even following his death, Davy Crockett became growingly famous for exploits of legendary magnitude.

1. Coordinated flight is defined as:

    a. The pilot applying control inputs that are suitable for the aircraft's density altitude.

    b. The pilot applying flight and power control inputs to prevent slipping or skidding during any aircraft maneuver.

    c. The pilot reducing back pressure on the control column or joystick while turning in the opposite direction of the horizontal component of total drag.

    d. All of the above.

2. In this paragraph, what is the meaning of the word *almanacs*?

    a. An almanac is a book of information including a calendar, weather based predictions, anniversaries, and important events that is published yearly.

    b. An Almanac is another name for a book of locally developed plays that is published every couple years or so.

    c. An Almanac is a series of comics based on popular folklore that is published every five years.

    d. An almanac is a name given to stories that are handed down from one generation to another orally, not by written word.

Rosa Parks was a civil rights activist who refused to give up her seat in the colored section on a city bus for a white person when the white section of the bus was full and was subsequently arrested. My

Story, which is her autobiography, she is quoted as saying, "People always say that I didn't give up my seat because I was [physically] tired [or] old... No, the only tired I was, was tired of giving in."

3. What is implied by the quote?

    a. That she was old and tired of walking home after work each day and finally gave in and paid to take the bus home.

    b. This quote implies that Rosa Parks was not tired physically, or too old to stand on a bus, she was just tired of having to give in to the demands of white people; she was tired of segregation based on race.

    c. This quote means that people thought Rosa Parks was just too lazy to give up her seat on the bus.

    d. Rosa Parks was just stubborn that day on the bus, and her actions had nothing to do with the civil rights movement.

One island from the shores of San Francisco Bay is often referred to as "The Rock"; Alcatraz Island. The island has been home to one kind of prison or another since 1861 up until 1963. During its time as a federal prison, it is stated that no prisoner successfully escaped from Alcatraz although there were fourteen attempts in that time.

4. Why were there never any successful escapes from the prison on Alcatraz Island?

    a. No one ever successfully escaped the prison because there were too many guards on duty. No man was ever left alone when outside of his cell.

    b. Alcatraz was inescapable because even if they penetrated the high-security around the prison, there was no way off the island since no boats were ever docked at the wharf.

    c. The entire premise of Alcatraz was that the men sent here were not to be rehabilitated back into society. Each and every aspect and component of the prison, the training of the guards, and the security around the rest of the island was created with the idea of keeping them on the island forever.

    d. The majority of men at the time the prison was active did not know how to swim, so those who attempted drowned in the water if they were not caught first.

When one wants to train a house-dog to ring a bell instead of barking to let its owner know it wants to go outside, there are only a few simple steps. First, when the dog is at the door, and barks take its paw and knock it against the bell that is hanging from the doorknob and only then open the door and let the dog outside. Repeat every time the dog barks to go outside. Eventually, depending on the stubbornness of the animal, the dog will cease barking at all and go to the bell and ring it each time it wants to go outside.

5. What is this type of training called?

    a. This type of training is called Negative Behavior Elimination Training.

    b. This training is referred to as either Classical Conditioning or Pavlovian Conditioning.

    c. This training called Positive Reinforcement Training.

    d. This type of training is called Basic Cognitive Retraining.

When we think of "rights" we think in terms of Human Rights. This refers to ideas that apply to everyone, everywhere in the world. These expectations are egalitarian and are part of a declaration called *the Universal Declaration of Human Rights* that adopted by the U.N. General Assembly in 1948 after the end of WWII.

6. In this paragraph, what does the word *egalitarian* mean?

    a. This word means that the rights contained in the *Universal Declaration of Human Rights* are to all be taken literally.

    b. Egalitarian means that ultimately these rights will also be applied to immediately to anyone and everyone who requests to be treated fairly.

    c. This word means that examples of basic human rights are included in the declaration adopted by the U.N.

    d. The word egalitarian means that Human Rights are the same for everyone, regardless of their race, nationality, or any other factors.

Each branch of the United States Armed Forces has special mottos that the soldiers live and are expected to die by. These special expressions are points of extreme pride for each member of the military.

7. What is the motto of the United States National Gua

    a. "This We'll Defend"

    b. "Always Ready, Always There"

    c. "That Others May Live"

    d. "Not Self, but Country"

Examples of colloquialisms include Facebook, *y'all, gotta,* and *shoulda.*

8. What is the definition of a colloquialism?

    a. Words that are only used by Americans who live in the south.

    b. Words that only uneducated people say.

    c. Words that are used in an informal conversation, not a more formal discussion.

    d. Words that have recently been added to the dictionary as acceptable words to use in the American English Language.

Lieutenant Hiroo Onoda was a Japanese soldier who was sent to a small island in 1944 as an emissary. He refused to believe that Japan surrendered in WWII until his commanding officer finally traveled back to the island in 1974 and finally convinced him that the defeat was real. He then returned to Japan and received a hero's welcome.

9. In this sentence, what is the definition of *emissary*?

    a. Emissary refers to Hiroo Onoda being an ambassador for the Japanese army.

    b. In this sentence, emissary means a secret agent or spy.

    c. The word emissary means messenger in this sentence.

    d. Emissary, in the context of this sentence, means a delegate of the Japanese government meant to establish an embassy on the island.

Milton S. Hershey was the founder of North America's largest chocolate manufacturer, now known as, The Hershey Company. It is hard to believe that, with such a large, successful business, that Hershey's first attempts in the confectionary business were such failures. After finishing a confectionary apprenticeship, he opened his own candy shop in Philadelphia; six years later it went out of business. He then returned home after failing to manufacture candies in New York City and in 1903 construction of a chocolate plant began in his hometown which was later renamed Hershey, Pennsylvania.

10. What is the main message of this passage?

    a. As an entrepreneur, if your first idea fails, do not give up, but move on to your next plan for success.

    b. One can only be successful in starting a flourishing business with the support of your hometown.

    c. It is more successful to manufacture chocolate than candy.

    d. If you start a worldwide profitable business in your hometown, they will rename the town in your honor.

"Beware the leader who bands the drums of war in order to whip the citizenry into a patriotic fervor, for patriotism is indeed a double-edged sword." This quote of Caesar's is completely anachronistic.

11. What does *anachronistic* mean in this context?

    a. This word means stolen in this sentence. This is a quote from another ruler from the time of Caesar, but not Caesar himself.

    b. Anachronistic means a quote that is pieced together from parts of speeches made by an individual. It is, therefore, a quote without any real meaning.

    c. In this sentence, the word anachronistic means that this is a true and accurate quote; not a paraphrase.

    d. The word anachronistic is defined as a quote that is not historically accurate in its context. At the time of Caesar; there were no drums of war, for example.

"A stitch in time saves nine." This is a proverbial expression that has been used for hundreds of years.

12. What is this phrase referring to?

  a. This expression means that there is a "rip" of some sort in time and space and that only by repairing this rip will we save the world.

  b. When this phrase is used, the person means that by repairing a piece of clothing, you will save $9.00 on replacing the garment.

  c. This phrase refers to a broken relationship. If it is not repaired in time, it will take years (maybe even 9 years) to mend.

  d. The literal meaning of this expression means that if you stitch something up in time, you will save 9 stitches later. In other words, if you don't procrastinate, and repair something as soon as it is required, you won't have a bigger or worse job to fix at a later time.

In the Shakespearean play, *Julius Caesar*, a soothsayer calls out to Caesar with the following quote; "Beware the Ides of March!"

13. What is the meaning of the quote?

  a. The soothsayer was warning the ruler of his impending betrayal and death at the hands of some of his most trusted men.

  b. This phrase was actually warning the crowd, not Caesar that on ever Ides of March the ruler must choose one human sacrifice to offer up to the Roman gods to guarantee prosperity for the coming year.

  c. The Ides of March was a day of celebration in the Roman Empire to commemorate the deaths of the Christians in the Coliseum. The soothsayer was merely thanking Caesar for the day of celebration. The word "Beware" has been shown to be translated incorrectly into English.

  d. The soothsayer meant to warn Caesar not to upset or anger the god for whom the month of March was named; Mars, the god of war. To upset the god Mars, was to ensure plague, famine, or other ruin.

Tornados occur when air begins to rotate and comes into contact with both the earth and a cloud at the same time. Although the size and shape of tornados vary widely, one can usually see a funnel stretching from the sky down to land. Most tornados are accompanied with winds as fast as 110 miles per hour and extreme ones can have winds as fast as 300 miles per hour.

The path of a tornado is hard to predict, but it is becoming possible to detect them just before or as they form with the continued collection of data through radar and "storm chasers".

14. Storm chasing is a dangerous profession so why do people continue to put their lives in danger this way?

    a. Storm Chasers are an interesting breed of people who seek the thrill and adventure that comes along with this profession, much like extreme sports.

    b. News channels will pay large sums of money for good video of tornados, so, although it is a dangerous profession, the money is worth the risk.

    c. It is very important to discover as much as possible about how tornados work so that ultimately, scientists will detect them earlier and give people more advanced warning to get to safety. More advanced warning is the only way more lives will be saved.

    d. For statistics reasons, it is important to get first-hand data during a tornado. This way they can be compared to other natural disasters such as hurricanes and tsunamis.

"Secret Santa Sings Special Song for Sweetheart" is an example of alliteration.

15. What does *alliteration* mean?

    a. Alliteration means that the sentence has more than one meaning.

    b. Alliteration means that people with a stutter would have difficulty saying this sentence.

    c. Alliteration means that most of the words in the sentence begin with the same letter.

    d. In this sentence, *alliteration* means that a secret Santa literally sang a special song for his sweetheart; it means that this actually happened.

The Schneider Family was not your average family. Three generations lived in one house; Mom and Dad, four of their children, and Mom's parents who were well into their golden years.

16. The term *golden years* means what?

    a. The term *golden years* refers to the best years of someone's life.

    b. This phrase means that the mom's parents were old or elderly people.

    c. *Golden years* is another way of saying, when they were rich.

    d. In this paragraph, the meaning of the term *golden years* means that the grandparents were spending their years taking care of everyone else in the family.

Ali had been on the road for thirty-six hours straight to meet an important client and hopefully finalize a huge new account for his advertising agency. After checking into his hotel, he intended just to drop off his suitcases and go down to the restaurant for a late supper. Once he entered the room, however, the cozy couch beckoned him to relax and take a nap.

17. Which phrase is an example of personification?

    a. "...the cozy couch beckoned him to relax and take a nap."

    b. "Ali had been on the road for 36 hours straight..."

    c. "...and hopefully, finalize a huge new account for his advertising agency."

    d. "...to just drop off his suitcase and go down to the restaurant..."

18. Which is an example of an oxymoron?

    a. Three of the employees were <u>let go</u> due to suspicion of stealing money from the cash drawer.

    b. The <u>stormy night</u> was perfect for this woman's current mood.

    c. It was <u>raining cats and dogs</u> when the school bell rang.

    d. The community center was collecting <u>useless treasures</u> for their upcoming garage

---

Between April 1860 and October 1861 The Pony Express delivered mail, news, and other forms of communication from Missouri across the Great Plains, through the Rocky Mountains, through the desert lands of Nevada to California, using only man and horse power. The Pony Express closed in October of 1861; just two days after the transcontinental telegraph reached Salt Lake City, therefore, connecting Omaha, and Nebraska to California. Other telegraph lines connect many other cities along the Pony Express Route.

19. Why did the Pony Express close?

    a. The Civil War stopped them from running their business.

    b. Another company was faster and took over the business.

    c. The Pony Express riders were unable to pass through the Rocky Mountains in the winter months.

    d. With the transcontinental telegraph connecting so many cities along the route, the Pony Express became redundant.

Between 1914 and 1935, George Herman "Babe" Ruth Jr. was known as "the Bambino" to baseball fans. Over his 22 seasons, he only played for three teams (Boston Red Sox, New York Yankees, and Boston Braves) and was known most for his hitting skills and RBI's statistics. Due mostly to Babe Ruth's hitting ability baseball changed during the 1920's from a fast-playing game with lower scores to one of higher scores and a slower pace.

20. How did "The Bambino's" hitting skills and RBI's statistics affect the way baseball was played?

    a. He hit so many batters in that the game went faster.

    b. The innings lasted longer with so many batters scoring runs.

    c. They had to stop the game because every time Babe Ruth hit a home run fans mobbed him.

    d. The Regulations changed which caused the game to last longer.

Kraft Macaroni and Cheese goes by many names. In Canada, it is called Kraft Dinner and in the United Kingdom it is known as Cheesy Pasta. No matter what name it is called by, this pasta dish has been a staple of the typical North American diet since its beginning in 1937. James Lewis Kraft, a Canadian living in Chicago struck gold by introducing this product during WWII, when more and more women were working outside of the home, milk and other dairy foods were rationed and hearty "meatless" meals were relied upon.

21. Why has this product continued to be a staple in our diet over seventy-five years after it was introduced to Americans?

    a. Most Americans love pasta and cheese.

    b. It is still the cheapest pasta on the market.

    c. The same factors that made its introduction so popular still exist today.

    d. It is still popular today because of brilliant marketing strategies.

Mathematics Knowledge

1. $\frac{4}{5} \div$ ___ = 2.

   Which of the following will fill in the blank?

   a. $\frac{2}{5}$

   b. $\frac{5}{2}$

   c. $\frac{1}{5}$

   d. Both A and C

2. {2, 4, 6, 8... 50}

   How many numbers in the given set are completely divisible by 3?

   a. 6

   b. 8

   c. 7

   d. 9

3. What will be the area of the shaded region in the below figure?

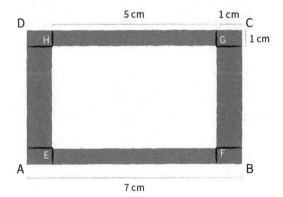

   a. 24 cm²

   b. 26 cm²

   c. 23 cm²

   d. 28 cm²

4. If $2x - y + 6 = 2$ then what will be the value of $6x$?

    a. $3y + 12$

    b. $y - 12$

    c. $y + 12$

    d. $3y - 12$

5. A point is located in a coordinate system at (1, 2). What will be the location of this point if it is shifted 5 units downwards and 3 units in the right direction?

    a. $(6, -1)$

    b. $(-4, 5)$

    c. Remains the same

    d. $(4, -3)$

6. $\dfrac{y+2}{3y^2+2y} + \dfrac{2y-1}{6y^3+4y^2} =$

    a. $\dfrac{2y^2+6y-1}{6y^3+4y^2}$

    b. $\dfrac{2y^2+8y-1}{6y^3+4y^2}$

    c. $\dfrac{2y^2+6y-1}{3y^2+2y}$

    d. $\dfrac{2y^2+8y-1}{3y^2+2y}$

7. Each side of a square has been increased by 1 cm and the area has now become 36cm^2. What was the length of one side of the square before it was increased?

    a. 4 cm

    b. 5 cm

    c. 6 cm

    d. 7 cm

8. $(9)^{-3} =$

    a. $\dfrac{1}{9}$

    b. $-\dfrac{1}{(9)^3}$

    c. $\dfrac{1}{(9)^{-3}}$

    d. $\dfrac{1}{(9)^3}$

9. What is the degree of polynomial $5x^2y - 5x^2y^2 + 5x^3y^2$?

    a. 12

    b. 4

    c. 8

    d. 5

10. Which one of the following numbers is not divisible by 3?

    a. 2352

    b. 3243

    c. 6143

    d. 5232

11. $(3 - x)(3 + x) =$

    a. $9 - x^2$

    b. $x^2 - 9$

    c. $9 + x^2$

    d. $x^2 - 6x + 9$

12. Which of these are parallel lines?

    a. $y = x + 5, y = -x + 5$

    b. $y = 2x + 3, y = 2x + 5$

    c. $y = 3x + 4, y = 2x + 4$

    d. $y = 4, x = 5$

13. Which of these are complimentary angles?

    a. 63 and 29 degrees

    b. 56 and 38 degrees

    c. 33 and 57 degrees

    d. 46 and 49 degrees

14. The triangle whose one angle is greater than 90 degrees is called

    a. equilateral triangle

    b. isosceles triangle

    c. scalene triangle

    d. obtuse triangle

15. $a \times (b + c) =$

    a. $ab + bc$

    b. $cb + ac$

    c. $ab + ac$

    d. abc

16. Which of the following is true for equilateral triangles?

    a. They have three congruent angles.

    b. They have three congruent sides.

    c. They have two congruent angles.

    d. Both A and B are correct.

17. If $\frac{20-x}{4} = 3y$. What is x in terms of y?

    a. $20 - 12y$

    b. $20 + 12y$

    c. $12 - 20y$

    d. $12 + 20y$

18. For which of the following functions does $f(x) = |f(x)|$ for every value of x?

    a. $f(x) = 3 - x$

    b. $f(x) = 2x + x^2$

    c. $f(x) = x^3 + 1$

    d. $f(x) = x^2 + (2 - x)^2$

19. . If $y = 7x$ and $x = 3z$, what is the value of y if $z = 2$?

    a. 40

    b. 44

    c. 48

    d. 42

20. $4\frac{4}{6} + 2\frac{1}{3} - 1\frac{3}{4} \times 3\frac{2}{5} =$

    a. $\dfrac{22}{20}$

    b. $\dfrac{24}{20}$

    c. $\dfrac{21}{20}$

    d. $\dfrac{25}{20}$

21. Which one of the following options shows the correct answer of y with respect to its equation?

    a. If $2(y - 1) + 6 = 0$, then $y = 2$

    b. If $3(y - 3) = 3$, then $y = 4$

    c. If $2(y + 2) = 6$, then $y = -1$

    d. If $6y - 18 = 6$, then $y = 5$

22. $A = x^2 + 3x - 4$, $B = 2x^2 - 2x + 3$. What will be the value of $B - A$?

    a. $x^2 - 5x + 7$

    b. $3x^2 - x - 1$

    c. $x^2 - 3x + 7$

    d. $x^2 - 5x - 7$

23. Pythagorean Theorem is applicable to which one of the following triangles?

    a. equilateral triangle

    b. acute triangle

    c. obtuse triangle

    d. right-angle triangle

24. $x = 3$ is the solution of which of the following equations?

    a. $6(x + 3) - 12 = 0$

    b. $8(x - 2) - 4 = 0$

    c. $7(x - 6) + 21 = 0$

    d. $3(x + 4) - 9 = 0$

25. There are two parallel lines, x and y. Line s is passing through both these parallel lines such that $<smk = 60$ degrees. What will be the value of angle k?

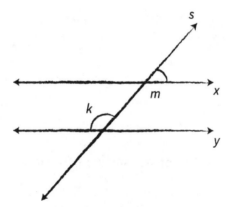

    a. 120 degrees

    b. 60 degrees

    c. 80 degrees

    d. 150 degrees

26. What will be the product of $3p^3 - 2p^2 + p$ and $-2p$?

    a. $-6p^4 + 4p^3 - 2p^2$

    b. $6p^4 - 4p^3 + 2p^2$

    c. $-6p^3 + 4p^2 - 2p$

    d. $6p^4 + 4p^3 - 2p^2$

27. There are two numbers, x and y, such that $x + y = 15$, $x - y = 3$. What will be the numbers?

    a. $x = 8, y = 5$

    b. $x = 10, y = 7$

    c. $x = 8, y = 7$

    d. $x = 9, y = 6$

28. $\dfrac{4}{5} \div \dfrac{6}{7} \times \dfrac{1}{2} + \dfrac{3}{2} =$

    a. $\dfrac{56}{30}$

    b. $\dfrac{57}{30}$

    c. $\dfrac{58}{30}$

    d. $\dfrac{59}{30}$

29. What will be the value of $x^3 + 6x^2 + 12x + 16$ when $x = -2$?

    a. 8

    b. 24

    c. 48

    d. 72

30. $6x^2 + 7y = 45$. What is the value of y if $x = 2$?

    a. 4

    b. 1

    c. 2

    d. 3

Mechanical Comprehension

1. *P* is a block of mass 5 kg. At point *Q*, a block of mass 3kg was attached just to slide the block *P*.

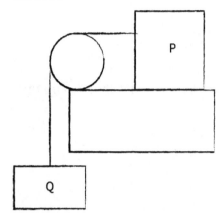

   If no displacement occurs, the coefficient of friction between the block *P* and the horizontal surface is:

   a. 0.5

   b. 0.6

   c. 0.7

   d. 0.8

2. A ball is thrown into the air. After few seconds, it returns back to the earth. What can be its likely cause?

   a. Earth's gravitational field pulls it back

   b. Its speed did not match the escape velocity of earth

   c. Neither of these is correct

   d. Both (a) and (b) are correct

3. The factor which distinguishes between a scalar and a vector quantity is:

   a. Magnitude

   b. Direction

   c. Both (a) & (b)

   d. Neither (a) nor (b)

4. An athlete couldn't stop himself immediately after crossing the finish line. He was explained why this was happening by Newton's:

    a. 1st law of motion

    b. 2nd law of motion

    c. 3rd law of motion

    d. Law of Universal Gravitation

5. How is the weight of a person in an elevator affected if the elevator accelerates upwards, accelerates downwards and is at rest?

    a. Increases, Decreases, Remains Constant

    b. Decreases, Remains Constant, Increases

    c. Remains Constant, Increases, Decreases

    d. Decreases, Increases, Remains Constant

6. In the above problem with an elevator, which of Newton's law is demonstrated?

    a. 1st law of motion

    b. 2nd law of motion

    c. 3rd law of motion

    d. Law of Universal Gravitation

7. The threads of a screw work on the principle of another type of simple machine, which is:

    a. Lever

    b. Inclined plane

    c. Wedge

    d. None of the above

8. The shaft of the screw penetrates wood through the principle of yet another simple machine, which is:

   a. Inclined plane

   b. Lever

   c. Wedge

   d. None of the above

9. The following objects are an example of which order of the lever:

   Forceps, Scissors, Fishing Rod, Bottle Opener

   a. 3rd, 2nd, 3rd, 1st

   b. 2nd, 3rd, 1st, 3rd

   c. 3rd, 1st, 3rd, 2nd

   d. 1st, 3rd, 2nd, 3rd

10. A mechanic observes that he is able to lift the car by 2cm if he moves the lever down by 30cm. if he is applying a force of 20N to the lever, the force applied by the lever on the car is:

    a. 250N

    b. 300N

    c. 350N

    d. 400N

11. Angular momentum of a body doesn't change if:

    a. External torque is not applied

    b. External torque is applied in CW Direction

    c. External torque is applied in CCW Direction

    d. External torque has no effect on the angular momentum of the body

12. Two moving bodies *A* and *B* possess the same amount of kinetic energy (see figure).

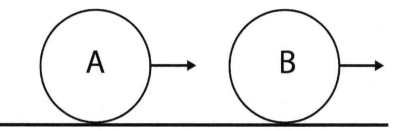

If both the bodies are of unit mass then,

    a. Velocity of body A > Velocity of body B

    b. Velocity of body A = Velocity of body B

    c. Velocity of body A < Velocity of body B

    d. Cannot be determined, insufficient data

13. A flywheel, initially at rest, attains an angular velocity of 600rad/s in 15sec. Assuming constant angular acceleration, the angular displacement and angular acceleration of the flywheel in this time is:

    a. 4500rad, 40rad/s^2

    b. 5400rad, 40rad/s^2

    c. 4000rad, 45rad/s^2

    d. 4000rad, 54rad/s^2

14. The wedge angle of a particular wedge is increased. The Mechanical Advantage of the wedge:

    a. Increased

    b. Decreased

    c. Remained constant

    d. Any of the possibilities is likely as M.A. is not affected by the wedge angle

15. Calculate the Mechanical Advantage of the following wedge:

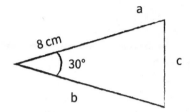

    a. 1

    b. 2

    c. 3

    d. 4

16. Observe the following figure:

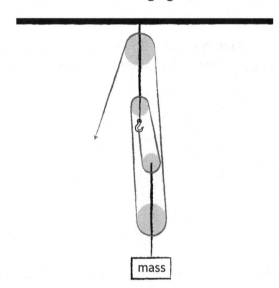

The mechanical advantage (IMA) for this frictionless pulley is:

    a. 3

    b. 4

    c. 5

    d. Cannot determine due to insufficient data

17. A body even after applying a certain amount of force, did not move. What can be said about the frictional force acting on the body?

    a. Less than µmg

    b. More than µmg

    c. Equal to mg

    d. Equal to µmg

18. The gravitational force exerted by one object on another at macroscopic level:

    a. Increases with the increase in distance

    b. Decreases with the increase in distance

    c. Remains constant

    d. None of the above

19. The dimensional formula of Gravitational constant is:

    a. ML^2T^{-2}

    b. $M^{-1}L^3T^{-1}$

    c. $M^{-2}L^2T^{-2}$

    d. $M^{-1}L^3T^{-2}$

20. A fighter jet traveling at a speed of 630kmph drops a bomb 8 seconds before crossing over a target to accurately hit the target. Identify the target of the jet.

    a. 1.2 km

    b. 1.4 km

    c. 1.6 km

    d. 1.8 km

21. Which of the following is not an equation of uniformly accelerated motion:

    a. $a = v^2 - u^2/2s$

    b. $a = 2(s - ut)/t^2$

    c. $a = 2s - ut/t^2$

    d. $a = v - u/t$

22. Newton's 1st law of motion is based on the Galileo's law of inertia. Which of the following types of inertia satisfy this law:

    a. Inertia of Rest

    b. Inertia of Motion

    c. Inertia of Direction

    d. All of the above

23. Observe the figure below:

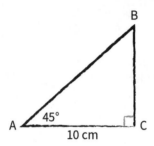

    The Mechanical Advantage of the given ramp is:

    a. 1.41

    b. 0.141

    c. 14.14

    d. None of the above

24. Which of the following is not a part of the incline plane family of simple machines?

    a. Wedge

    b. Ramp

    c. Lever

    d. Screw

25. The mechanical advantage of a screw having 6 threads per inch and a radius of 0.1in is:

    a. 3.33

    b. 3.55

    c. 3.77

    d. 3.99

26. Effort is being put on a lever with a speed of 20cm/s at a distance of 2m from the fulcrum. The speed at which the load moves, if it is located at a distance of 50cm from the fulcrum is:

   a. 80 cm/s

   b. 100 cm/s

   c. 120 cm/s

   d. 140 cm/s

27. Calculate the amount of work done in moving a mass of 10kg at rest with a force of 5N in 8 seconds with no repulsive forces in action?

   a. 80J

   b. 100J

   c. 120J

   d. 60J

28. Consider 3 equal masses at arbitrary points A, B & C in space and let D be a point on the surface of the earth (as shown in the figure).

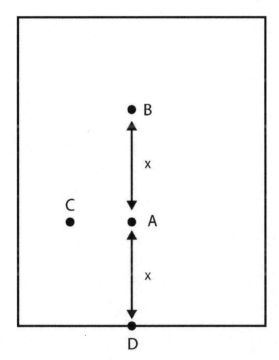

Then,

i. The mass at point B has the maximum potential energy

ii.   Masses at points A & C have equal P.E. but less than that of the mass at point D

iii.   The mass at point D, if lifted to a height 2x, will possess P.E. equal to P.E(B.

   a.   Statements (i), (ii) & (iii) are true

   b.   Only statements (i) & (iii) are true

   c.   None of them is true

   d.   Only statements (i) is true

29. The disc in the figure is set to roll with angular velocity omega.

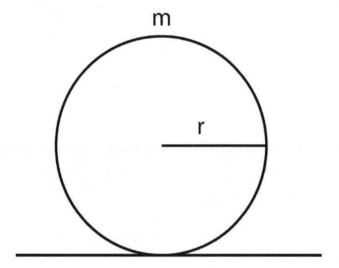

Total energy of the disc is:

   a. $(1/2)mr^2w^2$

   b. $(3/4)mrw^2$

   c. $(1/2)mr^2$

   d. $(3/4)mr^2 w^2$

Aviation and Nautical Information

1. An airfoil stalls when:

   a. The downward component of the wingtip vortices is greater than the lift produced by increasing the angle of attack.

   b. There is a rapid decrease in lift caused by an excessive angle of attack and airflow separating from an airfoil's upper surface.

   c. The pilot has mistakenly extended the flaps while flying above the maneuvering airspeed (Va).

   d. The pilot deploys the air brakes.

2. A propeller with a blade angle that can be changed by the pilot is called a _____ propeller.

   a. dynamic

   b. rotational

   c. reverse thrust

   d. controllable

3. The attribute of rotating bodies to manifest movement ninety degrees in the direction ofrotation from the point where a force is applied to the spinning body is called:

   a. Rotational precession.

   b. Dynamic precession.

   c. Induced precession.

   d. Gyroscopic precession.

4. An aircraft's initial tendency relative to its longitudinal axis after being disturbed anddropping a wing to return to level flight is known as:

   a. Lateral stability.

   b. Longitudinal stability.

   c. Directional stability.

   d. None of the above.

5. An imaginary line from an airfoil's leading edge to its trailing edge that is halfway betweenthe airfoil's upper and lower surfaces is the:

    a. Mean camber line.

    b. Chord line.

    c. Angle of incidence.

    d. Elevator inclination line.

6. When one surface of an airfoil has a specific curvature that the opposite side does not have, the airfoil is described as:

    a. Non-cambered.

    b. Deflected.

    c. Non-symmetrical.

    d. Laterally torqued.

7. The phenomenon of a propeller-driven aircraft's tendency to yaw to the left when the propeller rotates clockwise (as seen by the pilot) because the descending propeller blade on the right produces more thrust than the ascending blade on the left is known as:

    a. Asymmetric thrust.

    b. Rotational precession.

    c. P-factor (precession factor).

    d. Directional instability.

8. Airflow parallel and opposite to an aircraft's flight path is called the:

    a. Relative wind.

    b. Longitudinal wind.

    c. Dynamic wind.

    d. None of the above.

9. The speed of sound varies with:

   a. Angle of attack.

   b. Angle of inclination.

   c. Induced drag.

   d. Altitude.

10. A propeller-driven airplane tends to roll in the opposite direction of the propeller's rotation because of:

   a. The induced plane of rotation.

   b. Tangential drag.

   c. Torque.

   d. Angular momentum.

11. The starboard side of a ship is:

   a. Front

   b. Back

   c. Left

   d. Right

12. How many feet are in a Nautical mile?

   a. 5280

   b. 5500

   c. 6076

   d. 6676

13. What does Bravo Zulu mean?

   a. Well done

   b. Bring to the rear

   c. Be on alert for

   d. Repeat previous statement

14. What is the naval expression for a door?

    a. Door

    b. Portal

    c. Hatch

    d. Entryway

15. How many hours are in the "dog watch"?

    a. 1 hour

    b. 2 hours

    c. 3 hours

    d. 4 hours

16. The "Head" on a ship refers to what?

    a. The keel

    b. Aft

    c. Front

    d. Restroom

17. What is the proper term for a "wall" of a ship?

    a. Bulkhead

    b. Wall

    c. Divider

    d. Section

18. What is "Draft" on a boat?

    a. The water behind the boat as it moves

    b. How far a boat can travel once the propeller is stopped

    c. The depth of water needed to float

    d. The amount of speed due to wind draft

19. The "beam" of a boat is what?

    a. The overall height

    b. The width

    c. The section where the two sides of the hull meet

    d. The amount of hull under water

20. From what part of a vessel is a ship commanded?

    a. The bridge

    b. The Stern

    c. General Quarters

    d. Head

21. A helicopter is:

    a. A type of gyrocraft.

    b. A type of rotorcraft.

    c. A category of rotary-wing airplanes.

    d. A sub-group of gyrocopters.

22. Helicopter turbine engines produce _____ thrust per pound than piston engines:

    a. less

    b. the same

    c. more

    d. the same, but only after factoring in the effect of density altitude

23. The main forces acting on a helicopter are:

    a. Induced lift, mass, thrust, and form drag.

    b. Lift, weight, thrust, and drag.

    c. Lift, gravity, air resistance, and rotor vortex drag.

    d. None of the above.

24. Helicopters typically have between __ and __ main rotor blade(s):

   a. 2, 6

   b. 2, 10

   c. 3, 8

   d. 3, 7

25. Depending on the type of helicopter, main rotor system components can include:

   a. A stabilizer bar, upper and lower swashplates, and counterweights.

   b. Pitch horns, teeter or coning hinges, and blade grips.

   c. Pitch and scissor links, and control rods.

   d. All of the above.

26. The function of the flybar is:

   a. To decrease crosswind thrust on the blades and enhance flight stability by keeping the bar stable as the rotor spins.

   b. To increase crosswind thrust and modify flight stability by allowing the bar to spin at a slower speed than the main rotor.

   c. To decrease crosswind thrust and augment flight stability by maintaining the bar at an acute angle to the main rotor.

   d. To spin in a direction opposite to the main rotor's, thereby reducing induced drag

27. Many helicopters have a horizontal stabilizer located:

   a. On the mast.

   b. On the tail boom.

   c. On the fin.

   d. None of the above.

28. The purpose of the tail rotor is:

    a. To create kinetic energy that is transformed into potential energy as the helicopterclimbs.

    b. To produce rotational momentum that is used by the transmission to drive a generator.

    c. To produce an anti-torque force acting perpendicular to the helicopter's longitudinalaxis.

    d. All of the above.

29. Wheels on _____ types of helicopters are _____:

    a. all, retractable (to reduce drag).

    b. some, supplementary to skids.

    c. some, retractable.

    d. all, supplementary to skids.

30. A pilot controls a helicopter using:

    a. Flight instruments, hydraulic actuators, and a cyclic with a twist throttle.

    b. Flight instruments, pedals, two or more throttle levers, and avionics.

    c. Pedals, a throttle with a twist grip, collective link rods, and a cyclic.

    d. Pedals, and a collective, throttle, and cyclic.

Practice Test Two Answer Key

<u>Paragraph Comprehension</u>

1. A.

2. C.

3. C.

4. B.

5. A.

6. D.

7. B.

8. B.

9. A.

10. C.

11. D.

12. A.

13. B.

14. C.

15. B.

16. D.

17. B.

18. D.

19. B.

20. C.

Mathematics Knowledge

1. A.
2. B.
3. A.
4. D.
5. D.
6. A.
7. B.
8. D.
9. D.
10. C.
11. A.
12. B.
13. C.
14. D.
15. C.
16. D.
17. A.
18. D.
19. D.
20. C.
21. B.
22. A.
23. D.
24. C.
25. A.
26. A.
27. D.
28. D.
29. A.
30. D.

Mechanical Comprehension

1. B.
2. D.
3. B.
4. A.
5. A.
6. C.
7. B.
8. C.
9. C.
10. B.
11. A.
12. A.
13. B.
14. D.
15. B.
16. A.
17. B.
18. D.
19. B.
20. C.
21. D.
22. A.
23. C.
24. C.
25. A.
26. A.
27. B.
28. D.
29. A.

Aviation and Nautical Information

1. B.
2. D.
3. D.
4. A.
5. A.
6. C.
7. C.
8. A.
9. D.
10. C.
11. D.
12. C.
13. A.
14. C.
15. D.
16. D.
17. A.
18. C.
19. B.
20. A.
21. B.
22. C.
23. B.
24. A.
25. D.
26. A.
27. B.
28. C.
29. C.
30. D.

CPSIA information can be obtained
at www.ICGtesting.com
Printed in the USA
LVHW062153130321
681495LV00032B/571

9 781635 309683